GREAT PIANISTS SPEAK FOR THEMSELVES

GREAT PIANISTS SPEAK

ELYSE MACH

FOR THEMSELVES

INTRODUCTION BY SIR GEORG SOLTI
ILLUSTRATED WITH PHOTOGRAPHS

Volume 1

DODD, MEAD & COMPANY, NEW YORK

Reissued as a trade paperback in 1987.
No part of this book may be reproduced in any form
without permission in writing from the publisher.
Published by Dodd, Mead & Company, Inc.
71 Fifth Avenue, New York, NY 10003.
Manufactured in the United States of America.

1   2   3   4   5   6   7   8   9   10

Library of Congress Cataloging in Publication Data

Mach, Elyse.
  Great pianists speak for themselves.

  Includes index.
  1. Pianists—Interviews.   I. Title.
ML397.M28   786.1′092′2[B]   79-28736

ISBN 0-396-07824-9

ISBN 0-396-09213-6 [PBK]

Also by Elyse Mach

The Liszt Studies
Contemporary Class Piano
Franz Liszt: *The Familiar and the Unknown,*
   28 Pieces for Piano
The Well-Tempered Keyboard Teacher (forthcoming)
Great Pianists Speak for Themselves, Volume Two
(forthcoming)

You see my piano is for me what his frigate is to a sailor, or his horse to an Arab—more indeed: it is my very self, my mother tongue, my life. Within its seven octaves it encloses the whole range of an orchestra, and a man's ten fingers have the power to reproduce the harmonies which are created by hundreds of performers.

Franz Liszt, in an open letter to Adolphe Pictet, written in Chambéry, September 1837, and pub-lished in the Gazette musicale *of February 11, 1838*

ACKNOWLEDGMENTS

EVERY book is the product of the thought and work of many people, and I am especially grateful to those individuals whose generous help has made this book possible. Special acknowledgments go to Allen Klots, my editor, for his encouragement, pertinent suggestions, and professional expertise on the preparation of this manuscript; to Robert Silverman, editor and publisher of *The Piano Quarterly*, for his immeasurable help and advice on various phases of this project, and for granting permission to reprint excerpts of my earlier interview with Vladimir Horowitz, and an excerpt from Brede and Gloria Ackerman's interview with André Watts; to my dear friends and colleagues Anthony Brenner, Chicago City College, Ann and David Pope, Bowling Green State University, and William Schutt, Northeastern Illinois University, for their valuable help on the interviews and incisive comments on the manuscript; to the directors and staffs of the artist managements and personal managements, namely, Herbert Barrett Management, Herbert Breslin, Inc., Colbert Artists, Columbia Artists, ICM Artists, Judd Concert Bureau, Allied Arts Association, Alix Williamson, and Friede Rothe, for their professional support and invaluable assistance in arranging interviews with the artists and for responding so graciously to my requests for biographical information, photographs, and other data; to Robert Meissner, Kim Kronenberg, and Beatrice Stein, for their great assistance in contacting artists and procuring information and materials; to the late Harry Zelzer and his wife Sarah, for their generous help on the artist interviews; to Jerry Bush for his fine technical assistance; to Pauline Durack and Margaret Lynch, for their enormous assistance at home taking care of my three sons, Sean, Aaron and Andrew; to the members of my family, for their patient understanding and cooperation despite the inconveniences while this book was in preparation; and finally, to the artists, a very special measure of thanks for their generosity in granting interviews.

Elyse Mach

CONTENTS

ILLUSTRATIONS

TO AUNT LISA

INTRODUCTION

■■ ■■■ ■■ ■■■ ■■   by Sir Georg Solti   ■■■ ■■ ■■■ ■■ ■■

To attempt a definition of the nature of a concert pianist is to try to capture the wind. Some were born into a family of music, it is true, but few can boast of the outstanding pianistic abilities of parents or grandparents. Indeed, many overcame the opposition of a family to a musical career. Some began to show a musical preference almost as soon as they could walk; others developed somewhat along the lines of their physical maturity.

But all had something—the talent; it had to be there, because musical talent is something that cannot be learned. Such superb pianists as Chopin, Liszt, Rachmaninoff, Sauer, Cortot, Backhaus, to name a few—they all had it, and the artists in this book have it. No one can make a pianist like them because the mixture of pianist and musician is a marvelous, almost magical mixture. Anyone who is the least bit musical can learn to play the piano up to a certain point, but at that point progress ceases. The magic that makes the concert pianist or any instrumentalist is not there. For want of a better term, I call it a demon, a devil, a benign devil, but a devil nevertheless. Although a concert may last two hours or more, to the audience it seems like two minutes because they have become mesmerized by the demon that sits at the piano. Not every artist has it to the same degree, but each has enough of it to make him an outstanding pianist.

Given the talent, the prospective artist must have a firm determination to succeed. Some call it stubbornness, others, industriousness, but it's all the same. To achieve something you believe in is extremely important, especially for the young artist. An artist can always find someone who may not like him personally or agree with him professionally, but he must not allow such attitudes to affect his work or hinder his career. Criticism has to be overcome daily, and a truly good pianist will overcome it. No one can prevent true talent from its rightful destiny. Detours should only serve to make the talent more determined.

It should go without saying that the third ingredient is discipline which is the constant companion of the professional musician; and the virtuoso evolves from that daily practice. Moving the fingers up and down the keyboard becomes for most a daily battle, but one which constantly has to be won. There may have been a few exceptions to the rule, but eventually their absence of discipline caught up with them. The professional pianist can give performances without practicing maybe for a week or two, but usually no longer. As the Polish pianist and statesman, Ignace Paderewski, is known to have once remarked, "If I don't practice for one day, I know it; if I don't practice for two days, the critics know it; and if I don't practice for three days, the audience knows it."

As one reads *Great Pianists Speak for Themselves,* it becomes very clear that these keyboard artists did not rely on a miracle or good luck. They are men and women with talent who through industriousness, discipline, and belief in self-achieved stature have become the great pianists of all time. How they reflect upon themselves, their art, and their music should be very interesting indeed, for these are the thoughts of the artists themselves, not what someone else has chosen to write about them.

PREFACE

THE reluctance of famous people to grant interviews is understandable in the light of the number of misquotes, misinterpretations, and undeveloped generalizations usually attributed to them. Statements assigned notables are not usually distorted intentionally but, when one considers that the personage is questioned as he or she runs for a plane, leaves a stage, or enters a car, half-truths become commonplace.

The artists in this book gave several hours of their time so that they could add depth to their responses, especially in those areas that seemed most important to them. Since the pianists were quite communicative, it was decided to let them speak freely without prompting or interjection from the interviewer. Consequently, the reader will find little interruption in the artists' flow of speech. Question-and-answer interviews have their advantage, but they do not often allow the interviewee to develop his or her perceptions. While the danger of writer interpretation is ever present, by presenting the artists' views as they expand on them, the interviewer avoids putting words into their mouths. It is regrettable that tensions between the Western world and the U.S.S.R. curtailed access to the great pianists of the Soviet Union, and one such interview that was granted had to be withdrawn following recent defections by Soviet artists traveling abroad.

This book is intended for a wide audience because the artists themselves believe that their ideas and viewpoints touch all aspiring musicians, especially pianists, as well as teachers and music audiences. The parent who thinks his child has talent will note the various views on when and how to begin the youngster at the keyboard; the teacher of piano has the opportunity to study the influences of pedagogy, both in quantity and quality, on the student; and, perhaps most important of all, the serious piano student can clearly see what is in store for one who chooses the concert stage as a career.

Lastly, this book is intended for that vast group of aficionados of classical music whose appreciation of artistic skills brings them to the concert halls and to the record shops. How the virtuoso views himself, his art, and his public should satisfy the innate curiosity everyone has about famous individuals. The history of the talent, its development, and fruition will make even the dilettante more appreciative of the artistic accomplishments of these virtuosi.

Elyse Mach

GREAT PIANISTS SPEAK FOR THEMSELVES

Claudio Arrau

CLAUDIO ARRAU

Claudio Arrau has made his home in Douglaston, a New York suburb located about thirty-five miles away, since 1941. Mr. and Mrs. Arrau reside in a white frame house concealed by tall hedges. Mrs. Arrau greeted me at the door and immediately ushered me down a short flight of stairs to the large music room more conspicuous for its walls lined with shelves of books and objets d'art than for the black Steinway that occupied its own niche in a far corner of the room.

As Mr. Arrau entered the room, my curiosity about the total artistry of the room almost got the better of me; but as he began to speak I knew that, in his own time, he would explain why a music room was so filled with books, icons, African and pre-Columbian art, antique furniture and oriental rugs. Gentle and mild-mannered, Arrau speaks softly and slowly, delivering his carefully phrased ideas in an animated tone punctuated with much laughter and many gestures. Although he laughs easily, he weighs his words carefully, often stopping to rephrase a thought lest his meaning be misinterpreted. Like most other famous virtuosos, Arrau couldn't remember wanting to be anything but a concert pianist.

1

THERE was never a moment of doubt. When I look back, I think I was born playing the piano because, before I realized what I was doing, I was sitting at a piano trying out various sounds and playing in a very natural way. I had a feeling for the instrument. To me, even as a child, the piano seemed to be a continuation of my arms. On the other hand, natural gifts by themselves aren't enough. They have to be developed, and I was fortunate enough to be aided in my development by Martin Krause, who had studied under Franz Liszt. So I inherited the Liszt tradition, and through Liszt, the Czerny and Beethoven traditions. Krause was the greatest influence in my life because he was my one and only teacher. I may have had the same career without him, but it would have been accomplished much differently.

I know many artists claim they have developed by intuition, but I don't believe it. Intuition is important, so is talent. But a teacher, a guide who helps you unfold and develop is absolutely necessary. Also, that teacher has to be the right teacher for *you,* because the teacher-pupil relationship is a two-sided affair involving mutual responses. In a sense I worshiped Krause; I ate up everything he tried to put in front of me. I worked exactly according to his wishes. Krause taught me the value of virtuosity. He believed in that absolutely, but only as a basis for what follows—the meaning of the music, the interpretation of the music. Being a "piano player," no matter how brilliant, is never enough. I believe in a complete development of general culture, knowledge, intuition, and in a human integration in the Jungian sense of the term. All the elements, all the talents one possesses, should go into the personality as an artist and into the music the artist makes. Concentration should not be on music alone; to better understand music the artist must embrace, as it were, the total universe.

One of the most common criticisms leveled against musicians is that they are so specialized and that they don't live outside their own realm. The criticism may be valid, and I for one am very much against any attitude or philosophy that gives rise to it. When I teach, for example, I try to awaken not only musical elements in the young artist, but also to inculcate the importance of developing the completely cultured personality—reading, theater, opera, study of art and classical literature, even the study of psychology. All of these contribute enormously to making the complete artist. I myself, though I never went to school, was given the most thorough education. But mostly I continued to educate myself. I never stopped reading and wherever I am, I buy art of all kinds, as you can see. I need to surround myself with beauty. Art, beauty, nature, and knowledge are my inspirations. As for books, they are a passion with me. Not only this room, but the whole house is filled to capacity with books: modern and classical fiction, poetry, sociology, art, and musicology. I mustn't leave out books on psychology, one of my particular interests. Right now I am reading a marvelous new book, *Mozart,* by Wolfgang Hildesheimer. It's not available yet in English; it differs from so many books on composers in that it emphasizes the psychology of Mozart's music. Even television can be brought into the educative process. Although I'm far from being a television watcher, when I do hear of a very special presentation, I watch it. Just recently I saw a superb rendition of *Madame Butterfly* with von Karajan conducting. The music was beautifully performed and sung, of course, but it was the acting and the direction that made the production so different. What all of this means, or should mean, is that the true pianist must draw from all sources to develop his total personality. Not to do so is to remain narrow and incomplete as an artist.

Even if, for the moment, we confine ourselves to the study of music, I don't think it's a good idea to specialize in one composer. The wider you extend the range of your musicianship, the more every single composer you perform will gain. And if you're trying to learn a particular composition of one composer, it is extremely important to study the entire output of that composer so as to better understand his total language. Sometimes there are little enigmatic qualities in a composition that almost defy understanding until suddenly, through analogies in a piano sonata, in a string quartet, or in a symphony, what was vague before now becomes clear.

You ask how Krause taught me. Well, to begin with, he showed me the many ways Liszt used to play trills. He stressed the fact that trills had meaning; they were not merely adornments to a work but had expressive purpose. The trills had to be played at different speeds to fit the mood of the work being performed. Some were fast, some were slow, some were loud, and some were soft. The technique was determined by the character of the piece. And, in playing scales, arpeggios, and general passage work, Krause advised that the arms should be like snakes so that together with loose wrists there would be no interruption of the flow of movement anywhere. The whole picture was one of fluidity and effortless playing, whether you were rendering a great chord or the smallest package of notes. It is the way Liszt himself is supposed to have played.

Krause also spent time working with broken chords. He demonstrated how Liszt taught and played the big broken chords that appear in some of his études, for instance in *Harmonies du Soir*. And I can recall what he said about the use of the pedals. To get a very rich sound, but not a hard one, I learned to push the pedal down first before beginning the chord. However, when you sum it all up and talk of technique, you have to recognize that the apparatus is never an end in itself. Practicing trills, scales, broken chords, and pedaling is only the means to realize and express all your musical visions.

Technique is, to put it another way, the means to the art of interpretation. You have to start with an absolute faithfulness or loyalty to what the composer wanted by studying the early editions, the manuscripts and the facsimilies. If the composer noted that a passage should be played *fortissimo,* then it should be played *fortissimo,* not *pianissimo.* On the other hand, this fidelity and loyalty to what the composer wanted is only a basis on which the artist builds his own vision, his own idea of the work. But the vision must not jeopardize his respect for the text, or what he might know about the intentions of the composer. Some pianists "use" the original music and change it into a form of self-expression only. This is wrong. Others seem to be so awed by the composer that they do the opposite: They play nothing *but* notes. This is wrong, too. A good artist goes into a flight of imagination on his own, but he never destroys the integrity of the work as the composer saw it.

In no way, though, does this imply that the vision remains constant. As the artist's career moves along, he sees more depth; the vision becomes more profound. But it is a gradual process. You are always moving toward new revelations of the meaning of certain passages. And this brings you closer and closer to the core of the music. That's why it's inadvisable, for example, for a very young artist to want to play late Beethoven. He should occupy himself all his life with the study of the late Beethoven sonatas, but he should not want to play them too soon because that is an impossible pretension on his part. Works like late Beethoven and late Schubert should mature in you gradually. You should live with them for many, many years before deciding to play them publicly. This is also true of Mozart. In Schubert's early works, for example, there is the purity and simplicity, with some depth, of folk tunes. But in his later works I see what I call the proximity of death, death as a part of life. That mood is in the music and, most definitely, in the late sonatas and the late songs. Because there is such a combination of so many diverse elements in these works, I believe the young artist would have a hard time relating to all of them, not only because of a lack of life-experience, but also, as I noted before, because he hasn't come to know all composers and all the works of the composers.

Debussy is another composer whose depth and spirituality often escape the performer. Naturally, I think Beethoven is probably the greatest composer that ever lived, and the deepest, because he encompassed the whole cosmos. I'm sure he never realized how much meaning his works would have for future generations, and how those meanings might shift from time to time. But he must have felt something of the tremendous appeal that his music would have for many, many generations of human beings.

The music of Debussy, on the other hand, is something entirely different. The miracle in Debussy's music is this feeling of mystery, of musical mystery which makes it so difficult to explain what he actually meant. Again, one has to spend a lot of time studying his works before one really grasps the meaning of *his* meaning. There is no question about the incredible beauty of his sounds, but to stop at his sounds is to misunderstand Debussy. His sounds are the expression of more mysterious, more enigmatic, and very deep perceptions. That's why he is difficult to perform; his meanings present so many great problems. Ravel, for instance, is technically much more difficult to play than Debussy, but Ravel's meaning is far easier to grasp.

My interests, however, lie in the present, too. I'm very much interested in modern composers, but I have not had the time to study them very thoroughly. Had I the time, I would play a lot of their music. Names like Stockhausen, Boulez, Copland, Eliott Carter, and Charles Ives come readily to mind. I think Eliott Carter's piano concerto is a marvelous piece of work. Ives, of course, is almost a classic already; so is Copland. Arnold Schoenberg is another avant garde composer who will last, along with Stravinsky. And then I'd have to include a composer still unknown in America who has written an opera, *Die Soldaten,* which contains what I consider some of the greatest music ever composed. I went to see that opera three times when I was in Munich several years ago because I found it so incredibly filled with musical imagination and so rich in musical ideas that I could not absorb the total meaning at one time. Bernd-Alois Zimmerman died rather young, so his musical legacy is quite limited. But *Die Soldaten* will make him live.

Another modern whom I believe in very much is Michael Tippett. His opera, *King Priam,* is probably his greatest work. When I call it fantastic, I'm using the term in its strictest sense because the music in that work is so different from anything usually considered music. Both of them, Zimmerman and Tippett, go into realms that haven't been explored in music yet. The feeling I have about these two is somewhat akin to what I felt when, right after World War II, I heard electronic music in Cologne for the first time. "Now, what is this?" I asked myself. "This is terrific; this is tremendous; but what is it?" I couldn't put it into words because it was like listening to the music of another planet, or how one imagines the music from another planet would sound. So it is with Tippett; I could not possibly describe to you the realms that his music encompasses.

Yet there is still quite a way to travel. In Wagner's time the question was asked, "What can come after that?" But something did come. And after Stravinsky, they asked, "Who or what can come after that? Stravinsky is the end of music." But he wasn't. Ligeti, Berio, Penderecki, Carter, Zimmerman, Tippett, and others followed with new sounds, new depths, new visions. And there will be others still. There is never an end because there will always be new crea-

Claudio Arrau at five years when he
gave his first recital in Chillan, Chile

tions and for that reason it is impossible to stop. And why should it
stop? Thirty or forty years ago no one would have expected the flood
of avant garde music that we have today. "What could they do
now?" might be a valid question, but the proper artistic attitude to
take is to wait and to anticipate. Naturally there are and always will
be doubts, but something will spring up, be nurtured, and grow.

You're going to see changes in the performance format, too. I
don't think the recital, for instance, as an institution is at an end
because more young people seem to be interested in hearing live
piano literature and listening to it with greater participation. They are
so much more stirred up than the audiences we have been used to.
But the programming will change. We won't return to the potpourri
of a little bit of Mendelssohn, a little bit of Chopin, and a little bit of
Liszt. That arrangement has been pretty well used up. You may well
see more of what Mr. Serkin and I have been doing, namely, to perform three big works at one recital, or a one-composer recital.

As I noted before, the make-up of the audiences has changed
dramatically over the years. At one time concerts were almost re-

served for a standard of living rather than for people. And if one enjoyed that standard of living, the thing to do was to go to concerts. While at the concert, this audience was quiet, reserved, and appreciative. This is no longer true today. The audiences come from all walks of life. Recordings, television, and radio have made people much more knowledgeable about classical music, and they are much less reserved in showing their appreciation of artistry. They are much more stirred and are wonderful in their receptivity, in their openness. They enjoy, they clap, and they cheer. For many, too, the concert has become almost a religious experience, and this has led to an increase in participation.

I'm not so sure, though, that the product they receive is always that good. There are only a few artists today who give you musical depth. But then that was also true in the past. Who are the great pianists of the past most remembered? For me they are Busoni, Schnabel, Fischer, Cortot—all thinkers and great interpreters, as well as great pianists.

Today, too much commercialism has crept into the picture to allow the young artist sufficient time to develop. Music has become too big a business. Now young people win a prize and are expected immediately to live up to expectations. They are supposed to be ready-made great artists, which obviously they cannot be. They need time to mature; instead they are pushed into a tour of fifty or sixty concerts with only one or two programs, which is as unhealthy a situation as you could find. I suppose that, with the number of young gifted people available, it is quite difficult to make a career without winning a competition, but there ought to be another way, too. I know that Daniel Barenboim has never won a prize, but I think he is an extraordinary musician. To me he is the greatest of the young artists. In both fields, as pianist and conductor, he is really outstanding because he is a true musician. And while I'm on the subject of young musicians, a very interesting one to listen to is Martha Argerich. She is a bit inconsistent, but she shows provocative intuition in her playing.

Concerts still mean a great deal to me. Playing a concert has never become a routine matter. A concert for me is an event and, as long as

I look upon it as such, it will never be just a job. It has to mean something inside to the pianist; it's not just going out on the stage, playing some music, being applauded, and departing. The thing of it is, however, I never know just exactly how I'm going to perform. I suppose that is written in the stars. I'm always apprehensive and nervous before every concert, so the difference doesn't lie there. Through heavy concentration I overcome some of the apprehension; I also rest, or nap, for two or three hours in the afternoon before a concert. I try not to be distracted by anything and just prepare for the marvelous thing that *might* happen.

In general, I've cut my daily practice at the piano to a maximum of three hours. However, I do practice reading music a good deal. It helps me memorize a score quickly, both from the musical viewpoint and from the technical aspect. Of course I never immediately play a piece I've memorized; it must first be well digested by the unconscious. I believe the unconscious plays an important role in a performance. Many times it has happened that, while I was playing a concert, even though I had decided how I would play the work, some nuance, some turn of phrase crept into the playing that made the performance transcend what I had hoped for. I could have searched forever and never found it; yet it was there. Some psychologists say that this is the result of intensive work, a kind of serendipity; others claim that the ideas were lying in the unconscious all the time and merely needed triggering to bring them forth. All I know is that they were there and seemed to be almost metaphysical in their origins. They made for a most marvelous experience, as well as a frightening one.

What makes this all the more interesting to me is that, when I was eighteen or nineteen, I put myself under a psychiatrist's care because there was some kind of an emotional block that kept me from expressing my musical self. I knew I had to rid myself of this block if I was ever to be a concert pianist. I feared I was becoming neurotic over this problem and, because my career meant everything to me, I talked the whole matter over with a psychiatrist. He helped me dissolve the psychological difficulties I was having, and I began a phase of very rapid development. No major problems ever presented themselves again, but many times I continued to visit and consult this marvelous man just for the uplifting experience. I would advise any performer to talk things over with a psychiatrist and, if analysis is necessary, do it. The resulting peace of mind is worth it.

Critics, too, can sometimes point out problems in a virtuoso's style, but I think their influence is somewhat limited. One should be very careful in reading one's writeups because negative comments can lead to depression which is sometimes hard to overcome. I think that if a critic says something negative about an artist, the healthy thing to do is to consider it briefly and let it pass. Occasionally, one can glean a helpful thought, even if the thought seems inaccurate. I think it is healthier to know the reactions of others just to enjoy a certain peace of mind that comes from the satisfaction of curiosity. Some say they totally ignore critics because critics make them overly concerned about their artistry and this leads to constant nervousness.

I think the opposite is true, namely, that an artist can get too nervous from not knowing what is being said about him. In any event, I don't let them disconcert me, because frequently they are too inconsistent. I remember back in 1941, Claudia Cassidy printed nothing but raves about me. And then suddenly she began to rip me to shreds. Critics can be too erratic.

I don't understand why there are so few women virtuosos. There certainly are as many terrific women talents as there are men. Yet the field seems to be narrowed to Alicia de Larrocha, Jeanne Marie-Darré, Martha Argerich, Lili Kraus, Magda Tagliaferro, Rosalyn Tureck, and the Russian emigrés Oxana Yablonskaya and Bella Davidovich. So many start out with a tremendous drive, and all of a sudden they just drop out. They marry, perhaps, but that shouldn't be any reason for not continuing a career. Teresa Carreño was married four times, but she continued; and Clara Schumann continued her career after marrying, too. Perhaps the incessant travel today puts too much of a strain on their marriages. My wife was a singer, a very fine mezzo-soprano, but she never pursued a singing career after we were married. She has never said, one way or the other, that she regretted it, and I sincerely hope she hasn't. However, she does travel with me whenever she possibly can, more so now that the children are married and out on their own. But none of them is a career musician. My daughter used to play the clarinet, and play it very well, but she didn't want to practice and give it full attention. Apparently she wasn't born for it. Neither were any of the others, so I didn't push it on them. The interest wasn't there, so I never even tried to teach them. It might be that my absences from home made them think twice about pursuing a concert career, but I doubt it. If the spark is there, the flame will follow. A musician, just like any other career person, will make all the sacrifices to reach his or her goal.

In these later years I've slowed down slightly, of course, but even in the years of youth I wasn't always on tour. I've always loved gardening, and right now I'm planning new landscape designs to beautify our home in Vermont. I'm not very big on flowers, but my particular interest is trees, especially unusual trees that will flourish in that climate. I'll plant weeping beech, weeping cherries, weeping birch, and many fruit trees and pine trees. Now all this is done not just in the summertime when I'm not on tour; whenever I can get two or three days in a row, I'm off to Vermont to plant. So the career of a musician isn't totally devoid of outside interests. Besides, I'm fond of exotic foods such as Chinese, East Indian, and Mexican, so outside work is good for keeping the belly in trim.

You often hear musicians say that they would like to have lived in the age of Chopin, or Bach, or some other artist. Not I. Even if I had a choice of time in which to live, I would pick now. The questioning, the doubting, the nonacceptance of all the institutions and values that people have believed in for years are to me the marvel of our times. We are being forced to reexamine all of the traditions of the past not only in music, but in our general way of life. This is a fascinating experience. It may never come again, and I am glad to be a part of it. I don't believe in an afterlife, so whatever is, is right here and now. Consequently, one must be aware of the passing of one's life, especially the latter half of it which is actually a preparation for the end, for extinction. That is why I have stressed the building of one's own structure and one's own vision based on truth, on fidelity to the composer's text. That is my legacy.

Vladimir Ashkenazy

VLADIMIR ASHKENAZY

▮ ▮▮▮ ▮▮ ▮▮▮ ▮▮ ▮▮▮ ▮▮ ▮▮▮ ▮▮ ▮▮▮ ▮▮ ▮▮▮ ▮▮ ▮▮▮ ▮▮ ▮

The tape recorder and microphone seemed out of place in the lobby of posh Maxim's in Chicago but, since the patrons had not yet begun to occupy the crisp linened tables, Vladimir Ashkenazy didn't mind the peculiar setting for an interview. Immediately afterwards, he and his wife would leave for O'Hare Airport to catch a plane to the next stop on a tour that embraced 130 concerts a year. His full head of thick gray hair belied his relatively young age, forty-two; but, when one considers the decisions he has had to make, it is understandable that a physical change had to occur somewhere.

Although he defected from Russia in 1963, he is relatively apolitical except when he speaks of the relationship of freedom to artistry. Only then does he become somewhat voluble. Quite the antithesis of the men whose works he plays, Ashkenazy is generally quiet, unassuming, almost shy. By his own admission, he is not considered moody or temperamental. "I am usually quite constant; in fact, I'm pretty dull." Devoted to a work ethic, he is engrossed in music both at the piano and away from it.

ABOUT the only thing I do besides play the piano is read. I don't have much time for anything else. I believe, if you're going to be a success in this profession, you have to work hard at it. I realize there's no direct line between hard work and success because too many who worked hard never really had great careers; but when I've had a successful concert, when my playing has been well received, I have felt that much of it was due to my hard work. I still practice five to seven hours a day—some in the morning and some in the afternoon—when I'm on holiday in the summer or when I have a few days between concerts. The schedule of practice, however, varies greatly when I'm on tour because of travel connections, rehearsals, hall availability, and other problems that are connected with moving about. Nevertheless, all aspiring concert pianists should develop the work attitude and work habit. You'll often hear that competitions or sudden discovery are the routes to success. They may be at times, but you'll never even get to the competitions without hard work. And even if the competition isn't a great success, an individual shouldn't stop working at his piano because another route or opening may come his way.

Like many other artists, I was introduced to music at an early age in my home. My father is a pianist and I remember hearing him practice and listening to records when I was six years old. He wasn't and still isn't a classical pianist, however; he was an accompanist for variety shows which relied heavily on pop music. But that kind of music attracted me; I still think there's some good stuff there, although popular opinion might not generally agree. I used to sing many of the melodies my father played, usually the very simple ones, and my mother, although no musician herself, thought that I might have some musical talent. She asked me, even though I was young, whether I'd like to study an instrument. I said that I would and, since my father played the piano, it seemed only natural that I, too, should play piano.

Oddly enough, my father didn't participate in my musical upbringing at all. Even if he had wanted to, he couldn't have helped much because he had to travel a great deal and there would have been no continuity in his teaching. In fact, he never gave me as much as one lesson, nor did he find a teacher for me. It was my mother who took me to my first piano teacher. You have to realize that training in music is somewhat different in Russia. The conservatories don't take

Vladimir Ashkenazy with his wife Thorunn Sofia and his four oldest children: Vladimir Stefan, Nadia Liza, Dimitri Thor, and Sonia Liza

students until they are seventeen or eighteen years old. Before that comes ten years of training at a school of music. In my own case, I started my piano studies with a teacher when I was six years old and then, when I was eight, I continued my piano studies at the Moscow Central Music School for a period of ten years. All I can recall of that early training is Anaida Sumbatian, a wonderful teacher, working with me, to start with, on the technical aspects of piano playing such as scales, arpeggios, and especially the use of the fingers. I remember that sometimes she asked me to play with strong fingers and at other times to play with not so strong fingers. I really didn't pay that much attention to pedagogy, so my recollections of the early years are hazy. I simply followed the routine of the school and, by the time I reached the age of fourteen, I was playing some very difficult music, and she was wonderful with that as well.

By the time I was eighteen and had moved on to the conservatory to further my piano studies, I, like other pianists there, had a clear understanding of what had to be done. At that age any student should know what he lacks or what areas need special attention, and all the professors and teachers gave as much assistance as possible. It was too late, however, to work on fundamentals. The thinking was that, if you hadn't developed a certain amount of technique by the time you were seventeen or eighteen, you should forget about becoming a pianist. Moreover, the work demanded at the conservatory level didn't leave any time for work on fundamentals. The training there is difficult. Each student is expected to do all the most difficult pieces in the repertoire, according to his ability. A fragile girl, for example, wouldn't be expected to play the Rachmaninoff Third Piano Concerto. But the general level of repertoire is as difficult as it is high, and instructors presume the students will master it.

During those conservatory years, I worked diligently at my music to become as proficient as I could. While in my last year at the conservatory, I won the Chopin Prize in the Warsaw competition. It was the turning point in my life because winning the prize seemed to point the way to my future. Before that, I had played the piano simply for pleasure and for fun, and some of the fun was evaporating as the work became more difficult. Yet, it also became more interesting and my love for music increased proportionately. So, although until that point my life was a bit aimless, at least musically, now I knew that I would make music my career.

The approach to musical careers in the Russian conservatory is different from that in the schools of other countries. The Russian state is interested in winning international competitions because it is a matter of prestige. The collection of first and second prizes all over the world enhances their world stature, or so they think. They've developed a complex about it because they have to prove that their socialistic system is the best in the world; the "book" says so, so they have to prove it in practice. That's why they train their sports teams so strictly, and that's why they win so many athletic events. They train their musicians the same way, so they are very well prepared and win prizes. A famous American pianist and teacher I know remarked that Russian pianists are better prepared than most, but for me the question is, prepared for what? I tend to think that Russia creates good musical sportsmen rather than great artists. They play well, but I don't think they say very much. I can't remember hearing any young pianist who impressed me with something on the spiritual level. Their technique was proficient, but there was nothing more than that. They are imbued with a general spirit and attitude of great discipline, but that is characteristic of the whole country because the regime itself is so despotic. The pianist is disciplined to be first in competitions, but I can't say that he brings any fresh life to the music he plays. He is not developed as an artist in his own right, with an original outlook that communicates some special message. In general, young Russian pianists are very dull despite their technical abilities.

One mark of the Russian pianist is minimal motion. The arms and hands are fluid but quiet. Even as children, we are required to use as few movements as possible. We are taught not to waste energy. In my own case, the opinions seem to differ. I think I use little movement, but others disagree. Just yesterday I was asked why I use so many strange body motions. I'm not sure that all observers see or mean the same thing by "body movement," but I know we were all taught to be as relaxed as possible even though we were directed in the use of arms, wrists, and hands. I've heard it said that Horowitz, for example, plays with an outstretched hand, almost flat fingered, and that that is characteristic of the Russian school. In the first place, Horowitz is not the exemplar of the so-called Russian method. He studied in Russia at the turn of the century when regimentation might not have been so severe. Besides, he may have developed his own idiosyncrasies gradually without any direct attention being paid to them either by himself or by his peers. Secondly, even though there is this concept of a "Russian school," there are many different teachers and it is virtually impossible to keep all individuality out of their pedagogy. Consequently, any pianist might develop an individual style of playing based on what his teacher directed him to do.

I, too, think that Horowitz plays with flat fingers; I've never seen anyone else in Russia or any place else play like him. Yet when I see

Richter play, I also think that I haven't seen anyone play like that; the same is true when I observe Gilels play. I think they are all individuals; you can't categorize them. It's a dangerous undertaking, especially with the older artists. You also hear of the Neuhaus influence. But his influence wasn't as a teacher of technique; he couldn't teach anyone to play the piano very well because he couldn't play very well himself. His whole body as well as his hands were too small to generate any power. He did small Chopin pieces, some Schumann, and a little Scriabin exceptionally well. No one could touch him in that area. But he couldn't teach you to play some terribly difficult passages because the strength wasn't there, and he knew it. He recognized his limitations; he admitted that nature hadn't endowed him well enough physically to be a giant pianist. His pupils used to call him an eagle without wings because, although he had great mental capacity and knew what to do, his abilities were limited when it came to translating ideas into physical accomplishment. To save his life, he couldn't play something like the Brahms Second or the Rachmaninoff Third Concerto. But in artistic temperament, in personality, in musicianship, in inspiring others, he had no equal. He was one of my favorite people in all of Russia. It's a shame that a man with such a brain and such a personality was so handicapped by a small physique. Yet, he was a true artist, even within the Russian framework. Another favorite of mine is Richter, for today he is the most outstanding artist I know in Russia. He is genuine; he was born to it.

So, within the regime, artists can be developed despite the heavy weight given to uniformity because technique and artistry are inborn and, given time, they will sneak through the stereotype. Of course some technique is developed from scratch; even a dummy can generate some kind of technique, but only a born pianist will have a technique that is almost his second nature. Even when I was just playing around on the piano, I thought I had facility or dexterity at the keyboard. It's a matter of natural coordination, an action of the brain and a reaction of the nerves to the brain impulses. You're either born with this or you aren't. But the body generally must be in good shape, too; otherwise the impulses won't move the arm, wrist, and finger muscles as rapidly or as strongly as they should be moved. I was instructed as a child to play with strong fingers to develop them to receive the commands of the brain.

Generally speaking, the Russian technique goes over well with audiences because the average person wants an exciting and entertaining evening. About ninety-five percent of most audiences want something quickly accessible, attractive, and appealing. They don't require some transcendental spiritual revelation because such messages are not quickly accessible and appealing. An audience must be willing to think and be especially attuned to the depth of music to appreciate the images evoked by true artistry. But quick excitement is what Russian pianists provide, and it goes over well.

I don't think that's what art is or what music is about. The purpose of music is much loftier than providing mere excitement and entertainment at the physical level; yet I believe it's almost impossible to define what real music is. If you try to put into words what music is trying to say, then you have words, not music. This is why I play music; I have something I believe in, something I try to communicate, but I can't put it into words. So I play; it's my way of expressing what I cannot verbalize. Naturally this communication is much broader in the free world. It was the freedom of expression that I found in the Western world that spurred me to leave Russia in the first place. Until you've had the opposite experience, you'll never appreciate fully what it means to be your own master. First comes peace of mind, which is the most important attribute in a person's life. It is possible to attain it in Russia, too, but at a greater expense, for peace of mind entails refusal to compromise, and that requires unbelievable courage in the Soviet Union.

Secondly, for an artist to grow, he needs freedom. He must experiment, he must expand his repertoire, and he must use his powers of spontaneity. These qualities make music what it is, and in a dictatorship they don't exist, at least to their fullest extent. Often I'm reminded that I was highly successful in Russia; but success isn't everything. The freedom to try to shape one's destiny is much more essential.

After I left Russia, not only did I have to change as a person because I had left the country where I was born and reared and trained, but I also had to change my life style and the views on my art. We moved to London because, although my wife is Icelandic, she had lived in Britain for fifteen years or more. Wanting more privacy and less crowding, we decided to live in Iceland to enjoy its peace and solitude. We stayed there ten years even though, during that time, we realized that geographically Iceland is pretty far off the beaten path. Flying in and out became gradually more difficult as the number of concerts increased because between concerts I wanted to return home to see my family. This was impossible since there was only one flight a day which arrived very late in the evening; then I had to catch a six A.M. flight out because that was the only plane leaving. Consequently, I didn't really enjoy my free days. So we moved to Lucerne, Switzerland, which is much more accessible. My present schedule calls for approximately 130 concerts a year, but I can get to Lucerne much more readily than I could to Iceland, so now I have more time to spend with my wife and five children. I probably spend more time with them than most business people do with their families, especially those who travel. When I'm home I practice a lot but, as soon as the children return from school, I spend the rest of the day with them. When we travel, we take the preschool tots with us and, if I have to move about during their holiday seasons, those who are vacationing accompany us, too. In the summer, all of us take two months off and stay at a home we have in Greece. There's a piano there so I can practice my five or six hours a day, but the rest of the time belongs to the family. For us, this is a whole new way of life.

Naturally, I've changed musically, too. In the Soviet Union, the life of every individual is controlled as much as possible because the attitude of the state is that the individual is valuable only insofar as he is a contributing factor to the state or country. Consequently, his activities have to be controlled so that he gives only the service to the state which the state decides that he should give. Admittedly, the state recognized that the music profession is a relatively free profession in that there's no job to go to, no office to work in; on the other hand, it tried very hard to prescribe which composers we could play and which we couldn't. Twenty-five years ago, for instance, and for some years after that, no pianist could even think of playing Schoenberg, or Webern, or Berg. In 1951, I remember an orchestral concert in which Debussy's Nocturnes were performed, and I was informed that the conductor and orchestra had to get special permission to do those works. I'm inclined to believe it because, until that concert, I hadn't heard Debussy or Ravel or any composer in that idiom; and the entire music circle of the Soviet Union came to the concert since they hadn't heard such music either.

In Russia, everything is controlled by party ideology. In the twenties, for example, playing Tchaikovsky was forbidden because he was considered a bourgeois decadent. Suddenly the party did an about-face on the matter because someone pointed out that the prohibition was ridiculous since Tchaikovsky was Russian and, by omitting him from musical programs, the country was losing part of its heritage. So when you see what the Soviets did to Tchaikovsky, it's little wonder that they would prohibit the playing of Debussy because he isn't exactly a model of socialistic realism. Impressionism, as represented by Debussy, Ravel, and others, was taboo for some time because they didn't conform to party ideology. Gradually the reins were loosened on other composers, too, as the party came to realize that music is not so politically sensitive. Still, music in the Soviet Union is not as free as it should be, nor for that matter are musicians. No artist likes to be told what to do and what not to do. I still like to select my own programs, and I do it very simply; I play what I like to play—Mozart, Beethoven, Schumann, Schubert, Chopin, and Russian composers, of course. I try to put together a program that has a lot of variety, but harmonious variety. The selections are diverse, but the result is unity. In any case, the choice must be mine. If I want to play the Rachmaninoff Third, I'll play it; the same is true of Liszt's *Transcendental Études,* although now I don't find them particularly interesting so I omit them from my programs. Besides, since my hands are not gigantic, it's quite a struggle for me to do Liszt. And there's still some Schubert I want to learn along with other pieces of Schumann and concerti of Mozart as well as the works of Strauss. This season I've added Bartok's Second Concerto to my repertoire, and I'm in the process of recording all thirty-two Beethoven sonatas, something I've never done. I'm trying to learn new material all the time, not just because it's new, but because I can learn more about music and composers. On the other hand, I haven't done any of the avant garde material, and I don't intend to; I'm not interested in it at all. It may last, it may not; I don't know. I leave prediction to others.

I wouldn't mind, however, visiting the past if I could just meet some of the classical composers like Beethoven, or Rachmaninoff, or Chopin, or Mozart. I'm not sure whether or not I'd benefit musically from such encounters; to know a man's music you must study the music, not the man, although the composer can be of some help. Yet, I know I'd find the personalities of these men most interesting if for no other reason than to verify what we have heard about them. I'd like to separate legend from fact. Was Beethoven really as eccentric, abrupt, and temperamental as he is made out to be? Rachmaninoff is characterized as a gloomy person, very severe in attitude and appearance. Yet he's one of my favorite composers and, since he was also a great pianist, he would be a fascinating man to observe firsthand. I picture Chopin as a sophisticated, elegant, refined man, perpetually ill, but a genius in spite of it; I would like to see the difficult life of a genius close up. Mozart is very controversial. Some say he was beset with gambling debts and lost a fortune. Yet, other accounts of his life disagree with that point. Apparently, he was a disorganized person, especially where his personal affairs were concerned. It certainly doesn't show in his compositions. At any rate, I am curious about their behavior patterns, and I'd like to have my curiosity satisfied.

Besides having preferences for composers, I also have favorite places to visit and perform in. I particularly like England, the United States, Australia, and the Scandinavian countries. I don't think I'll ever play in the Soviet Union again, but that's only a thought. You can't predict anything about the Russians. They might change their policy for aesthetic or political reasons and forgive the defectors to the extent of inviting them to play again in their country; but by no means will this indicate a change in their total political outlook. Should the world last another hundred years, Russia won't change much because the government enjoys its despotic hold over the people and because everything there moves so slowly, just like a lumbering bear; any minor changes that appear will be superficial and will not affect the fundamental principles of the government. But predictions are dangerous and this is only a feeling based on knowledge.

In the meantime, I still have much work to do. As I mentioned, there's so much music that I have yet to add to my storehouse, and time is a factor. I can learn shorter pieces, like some of Chopin, in a few hours, or two days at most. But a Beethoven sonata will consume a week or two of my time. I probably know the work already in my mind and in my ears, but I have to get it into my system; it has to become part of me so I don't have to concentrate on which note to play next and which finger I use to play it. I don't do all my work at the piano, either. I try to let the composition run through my mind whether I'm on a plane, a train, or just relaxing. I don't necessarily have to look at the score because I don't have to see every note. I try to understand structural relationships and move through the piece slowly, especially if it's a difficult one. Then, at the piano, I just play it. I try to interpret the critical notations of the composer. *Forte piano* is always *forte piano,* but there are so many ways of rendering it that I have to find the one that convinces me. Sometimes, but not often, I deviate totally from the composer's marks because I'm not convinced that a section comes through firmly or clearly enough, and I believe I'm justified in doing so. One of the problems is the number of misprints that creep into the printed score; another is lack of precision on the part of some composers. In such cases, the artist is pretty much on his own. He must use the interpretation which seems right to him. Regardless of the composition, however, I respect the difficulty inherent in all music; otherwise there would be no need for so much practice. I want to be as sure as I can be that the music comes across as music. Working hard at practice is also the best defense I know against preconcert nervousness, which can never be entirely eliminated but can be psychologically prepared for by convincing oneself that one has done all the homework necessary for a solid performance and everything will work out all right.

The concert pianist must devote all his life and all his time to music. Style, technique, meaning, and interpretation are not accidental qualities that just seem to fall into place at a given time; they are the result of practice and concentration which comes only through a lot of hard work. It's the best way I know of gaining some measure of success.

Alfred Brendel

ALFRED BRENDEL

▌▐▐▐ ▐▐ ▐▐▐ ▐▐ ▐▐▐ ▐▐ ▐▐▐ ▐▐ ▐▐▐ ▐▐ ▐▐▐ ▐▐ ▐▐▐ ▐▐ ▐

On a hot, muggy July day in Chicago, native and visitor alike scurry from one air-conditioned place to another seeking some relief from the midsummer swelter. Certainly one would expect to find a visiting virtuoso comfortably resting in the coolness of an apartment or hotel suite. But not Alfred Brendel. Clad in blue jeans and an open-collared shirt, this tall and very lanky figure was taking his ease behind the stage of Murray Theatre in Ravinia Park. His face showed traces of weariness and myriad beads of perspiration studded his forehead, the result of his having just completed several hours of practice for an upcoming performance in which he would play three Beethoven concerti, a prodigious undertaking even in a cooler atmosphere. The slight weariness evidenced in his face fell away like a husk when he began to talk of his career, his love for music, and his preference for the piano.

IT was only when I was about seventeen or eighteen that I decided to make piano playing my profession. Until then I had been doing all kinds of things at the same time. Although I had begun to study the piano at age six, as time went on I composed, I painted, I read avidly and, of course, wrote poetry; so there were a number of roads which seemed open for a little while. Then I decided to see just what could be done with the piano, and it was the right decision. For, as I progressed, I saw that the piano is an instrument which constantly should transcend itself. As such, the piano sound is not terribly interesting or individual compared with the human voice, for example, or with a stringed instrument. It does not have their direct, sensuous appeal. It waits to be turned into something else. It waits to play roles, as it were. It should sound like anything else, but not like a piano. It should be an orchestra, or it should be a voice; it should sing because the singing line and the singing quality are so basically important in music. It can and it should evoke sounds of other worlds, but it should not sound just like a piano.

I was not a child prodigy; yet I did not have a teacher after I was sixteen. I merely attended a few master classes, of which Edwin Fischer's have stayed vividly in my mind. So I had to find out many practical things for myself which made it a slow process, but a process which was thorough and entirely my own. In the first place, I learned to look at each masterpiece as an entity in itself. One has to find out why a work is different and unique, much rather than why it is similar to other pieces.

Secondly, I try to look at each piece as naïvely as possible. I do not try to analyze it first. I think that analysis, becoming aware of the processes in the composition, should be the result of such acquaintance, not the input. So I become more and more aware of pieces the longer I play them, and yet I try to maintain the naïveté. Is feeling more important to a musician than thinking? As I have said in my book, *Musical Thoughts and Afterthoughts,* "As much as I enjoy thinking, I find that feeling is the *Alpha* and the *Omega* of the musician, the point where music comes from and the point to which it has to return." That does not mean that I do not value thinking very highly. In fact, I value it much more highly than most people seem to because this is one of the criticisms leveled against musicians and the nature of their music—that they should not be "intellectual" or else the magic of the music, its spell, is lost. There are too many people who would like music to appear as something which comes down directly from heaven.

Anybody who has ever tried to live with masterpieces of music for several years and become aware of what they are about, how they are constructed, how themes, motifs hang together in a movement, and how movements hang together in a sonata will discover that a Beethoven sonata is a tremendous intellectual feat and that the intellectuality of the sonata is an integral part of the whole. The intellectuality is tied to the emotions. It is really an interplay between chaos and order. According to the German poet Novalis, "chaos has to shine through the adornment of order" in a work of art. Without order there would be no work of art. If chaos is life which surrounds us, the work of art is something which puts order against it. So for me a work of art and life itself are diametrically opposed; they do not necessarily mirror each other. Consequently there are artists in whom you would not recognize the man and some men in whom you would not recognize the artist.

What it all comes down to is that I learned that the music dictates the terms. It tells you what to do with fingering, pedaling, and hand movements. That's why I do not believe in the intentional slowing up of the tempo in practice or in warm-up. If I slow down the musical process, the fingering may be wrong; the movements may be inadequate. On the other hand, to try to discover fingering by playing in slow motion a piece which goes rapidly is basically wrong. This is one of the qualities I admired in Edward Steuermann's teaching: He made his students learn passages at a fast tempo, but he subdivided the passages into smaller bits. He'd tell the student to go up to a certain place and play in a specific manner. Next he asked the student to play the second bit and connect it with the first, but not in slow motion. This went on until the student had finished the passage. This system may also be beneficial for memorizing the whole work. For some reason, I've never had a serious memory problem. Usually, after I've played a work a few times, it sticks in my mind. When I have memory lapses during a performance, they tend to occur in recital rather than with orchestra. Somehow I manage to work my way out of them as most artists do. Edwin Fischer, Alfred Cortot, and Artur Schnabel all confessed to memory failure at times, but they survived. I don't believe any of them would have deliberately slowed down the tempo of a selection in order to avoid the risks of running into technical problems when playing at the necessary speed.

To help myself along further in my pianism, I listened to performances by Arthur Rubinstein and Wilhelm Kempff. I am interested to hear my younger colleagues, but I profit most when I go back to old records of Fischer, Cortot, and sometimes Schnabel. Actually, I pay more attention to conductors and singers than I do to pianists. There is more to learn from them. Still, I'd like to hear Beethoven and Liszt play if I could. I think Liszt would be superior to almost any pianist today. He'd have more to offer musically. If you look at what he wrote as a young man, for instance, the most difficult version of the Études (*twelve études d'exécution transcendante*), then I could not imagine anybody being even technically better today. There may be some who would probably play fewer wrong notes, but so what? I'd like to have met Schubert, Beethoven, and Mozart. Mozart would probably be the most interesting because it is so hard to conceive what he was like. I don't suppose anyone will ever find out. I hope to continue to mature. I'm still in my forties, and there is much to be learned. Although I generally cannot complain about the reviews I get, once in New York a critic suggested that my playing of Beethoven would mature in the next few years. I hope the critic was right. I'm discovering new subtleties in Beethoven all the time. The awareness must be ongoing. I think it would be very sad if I thought I had achieved the totality of Beethoven. Because his works are so enormously complex, there simply is no end of discovery of new insights into his work. But I don't need a critic to tell me that. What the artist has to do is maintain his own judgment. He must not be too much influenced by critical voices. Sometimes the critic may be right, but it is usually in the area of how the concert came across. If I get the impression that I have not played well, it is often that some quality of communication was lacking. For instance, I may hear the sound much differently on the stage from the way the people in the audience heard it, and that will alter the whole projection of the performance just as the projection may be altered when you listen to the same record on different amplifiers and speakers. Sometimes a dif-

Alfred Brendel and his son Adrian in 1978. *Misha Donat*

ferent pressing of the same record may produce a different, disappointing result. Some place along the way an important point of focus got lost. One important question that I must continually ask myself is, "How did it come across? What did *they* hear?"

So when you ask about the nature of my success, or the success of any artist, all I can do is point out the complexity of the entire process and, at the same time, admit that it almost defies understanding. Certainly I had no early success to speak of. I was not the type physically to appeal to a wide public when I was twenty-five. I did not appeal to mothers, and I pulled a lot of grimaces. I was really a kind of outsider, and I wanted to be an outsider. I looked at the public with a kind of irony or disdain as a necessary evil; I never knew in those early years how to project what I did. I tried to work everything out on my own, so it took much longer for me to make a career for myself. The process, however, had some advantages: it gave me more time to learn repertoire quietly; it afforded more opportunities for me to learn about people; I could leisurely study the facts of concert life and observe how the concert machinery works, and I gained a better perspective into what I'd have to put up with as a concert pianist. Thus I was not under that great pressure of maintaining an early success which can ruin even big talents. I don't think there is any general recipe for success; if there is, I know I didn't follow it.

What the future will bring is, of course, as difficult for me to predict as it is for anyone else. I know I don't want to be a conductor. I'm enormously interested in conducting because it tells me which modifications of tempo a pianist should avoid as much as possible: those which cannot be conducted. I often conduct in my mind—and there my conducting will remain. There cannot always be a meeting of the minds of soloist and conductor on the performance of a particular work. Sometimes it's a matter of technique, sometimes of age differences, sometimes of personalities. In such instances one has to compromise to get, if not the ideal, then the best possible result. Sometimes, for example, a conductor thinks a composition should be played at a different speed. I try to talk him into my view of the piece, but it may not be convincing simply because he cannot feel it my way. Sometimes, too, a technical question is involved. For instance, in the first movement of Beethoven's Concerto, No. 1, which I am convinced should go very fast, it only makes sense in an extremely fast four. Now, to beat a fast four may be very awkward for some conductors. If they start it *alla breve,* the music sounds different. It's not what it should sound like—the first and third beats are slightly emphasized, the second and fourth slightly neglected. Similarly, Brahms's D Minor Concerto is a famous obstacle even for some of the most experienced conductors because the tempo of the first movement is just somewhere between the beat of six and an *alla breve*. When the conductor beats six, the movement may get too slow; when he beats *alla breve,* it may be too fast and imprecise.

I must say that most conductors try to be very cooperative, depending on the respect they have for the soloist. Conductors respect those soloists who know the entire work rather than the few notes they have to play. Problems arise with some older ones either because they do not have the urge to rehearse so much, or because they want to do their own thing. Once a conductor is past seventy, there's little good in arguing with him. The soloist might as well make up his mind to accompany the orchestra. I have found few exceptions to this; Sir Adrian Boult is a notable one. The conductor has to maintain his authority over the orchestra. If he feels insecure, he'll look on the soloist as a challenger, and the entire performance will sound like one person trying to gain superiority over the other. Claudio Abbado, Daniel Barenboim, and Jimmy Levine are among the conductors with whom I like to work because they understand what I want; another one is David Zinman, who I hope will soon be as famous as he deserves to be.

I'm not enthusiastic about teaching, although I suppose everyone expects a concert artist to be a teacher. It's not that I haven't done it; I have. There are basically two different ways of teaching: One is to build up a student over a long period and be totally responsible for him, not only musically but also psychologically so that the teacher is his confidant, his motivator, and his love-hate object; the other way is to teach master classes, to have brief encounters with people in which the focus of attention is the work, and only the work. I have never felt the urge to teach regularly. On the other hand, master classes have given me pleasure, depending on the level of the participants. There one can give a diagnosis to some degree of what the player has or what the player lacks. But I still insist on the player finding his own way out as I found my way out. I suppose that I assume all artists developed in this manner, and I may be assuming too much. In 1960, together with my Viennese colleagues Paul Badura-Skoda and Jörg Demus, I set up a plan to hold master classes for three weeks each year, the object being that the students would hear three different, even opposing, opinions about the same piece. Thus the students would have to make up their own minds about the interpretations and decide which to choose. This would have been a first step, at least for the more talented ones, in the direction of musical self-rule. Of course, there were always those who added up our information and concluded that, where all three teachers said the same thing, it must be particularly true.

I have no immediate plans to do any more teaching. If I have the time, I'm going to do more writing. *Musical Thoughts and After-thoughts,* which was recently published, doesn't even begin to cover all the ideas I have about music. Mostly it is a collection of lectures and articles written over the years supplemented by other articles amplifying, clarifying, or contradicting my previous views. Each of them is dated so that the reader can easily follow the chronology of ideas. Since they don't encompass my whole repertoire of professional experience, they are only fragments of what I would like to say in the long run. There are three rather long articles on problems connected with Beethoven's piano works, one article on Schubert's late sonatas, several smaller pieces on Liszt, three little essays on Busoni, and two on my teacher, Edwin Fischer. There is also an essay called "Coping with Pianos," which tries to explain the relationship between a performer and the piano. Strangely, very little has been written on this subject before. I try to show what pianos should be like, but often aren't, and how pianos could be improved. I haven't pursued painting since my teens, except as a viewer. To look at late Baroque and Romanesque architecture has become a major hobby.

My primary goal is, of course, to continue to play the piano. The repertoire is so large; there are so many pieces I want to live with and a number of others which I want to learn. I shall continue to live with Beethoven, whose piano works I've recorded many years ago. In fact, I've just completed a new set of his sonatas. Then I want to do more of the Haydn sonatas, and some Schumann which I have not previously played. For instance, I've never played the *Davids-bündlertanze,* and I've always wanted to do the *Fantasiestücke.* I intend to add some of Smetana's piano music which is unjustly forgotten. There'll be more Busoni, but not his concerto and the *Indian*

Fantasy. I'm not convinced by these pieces. The concerto is a period piece—of a period which doesn't interest me very much. There was a gap in his production and, after the gap, he produced what was really worthwhile. It started with the Elegies, seven in all. The first of the Elegies, "Nach der Wendung" (After the Change), seems to indicate that he realized his music was undergoing some metamorphosis. Whereas before he had been an eclectic composer, he was turning into an original one.

The music of the present and the future have to be considered, too. Some of the important contemporary composers are my friends even though·I don't play them (my repertoire stops with Arnold Schoenberg and Alban Berg). Actually, in my musical taste, I am a very progressive person. I don't like reactionary music, music which sounds as if I had already heard it before. Schoenberg, Berg, and Webern were great composers. I admire some of Bartók's music, too, though I am not so fond of his latest works. I prefer what he wrote up until the time he left Hungary. I think his First Piano Concerto is superior to the other two, and I prefer the Third and Fourth String Quartets to the later ones. But this is the new music of our grandfathers. I haven't the faintest idea of the direction music will take. I'm not pessimistic about it. The aesthetics of music have changed so much in the last fifty years; why shouldn't they continue to change? If music goes back to elements of the past they have to be rediscovered in a new context. Concert programs may change as well. Already that kind of recital which resembled a menu has been largely abandoned. In Liszt's day, there were mixed programs with orchestra, an aria, and a pianist doing improvisations, two movements of a symphony with another aria in between the movements, and other productions that featured a multiplicity of artistry. It is not likely, however, that we will often return to this practice, though I sometimes enjoy mixed programs. At the Promenade Concerts in London I once played the *Diabelli* Variations in an orchestral concert. And last season I did a performance of Beethoven's Sonata in E-flat Major, Opus 7, which I followed with the *Choral Fantasy*.

Playing gives me enormous pleasure, though at times it can be just plain hard work. There are days when I hate to play! It becomes an enormous effort. I may not feel well, or I may be tired, or I'm just simply not at ease. The weather might be bad and I sometimes react to the changes in barometric pressure. Sometimes it's the hall, sometimes it's the instrument I have to use, sometimes it's the program itself. Sometimes it's a mixture of all of these elements, and that's very frustrating. There are some works that I simply don't play any more because of the stress that has been associated with them. For some strange reason the memory retains the struggle that accompanied the playing of some pieces under unfavorable circumstances, so I refuse to fight against this burden unless I feel that I cannot live without the piece; then I try to overcome it. There seem to be artists who subscribe to the biorhythm theory. I don't. There are other artists who rely on their astrologer's predictions so intensely that they make all their important concert dates coincide with the astrologer's prophecy of success. It makes no sense to me and, even if it did, I wouldn't want to know what might happen to me tomorrow. If at all possible, an artist has to give his performance. He may have to fight his way through the program, but this is life. Such a performance leaves me totally drained. How different is the freshness I feel after a concert in which everything has gone well. I have no pet superstitions or good luck charms that will put the gods to my service. I prefer to be well prepared. My routine is simple: After I rehearse, I usually take a short nap; then, a half hour or so before the concert, I warm up to activate my hands. I wouldn't like to go on stage without having played a little. This system has worked rather well for me. I try to confine my practice to about five hours a day now. Any more than that I find not good for the physique or for the mind. I believe it is important to spend time thinking and studying the music away from the piano.

Another facet of this profession that I like is the travel. If I didn't, I probably would have changed professions a long time ago. I've had over twelve years of very active traveling, and I still look forward to it. Of course, while our two children are so young and not going to school, it's possible to take them along on tour sometimes. Once they start school, however, I intend to decrease some of my activities, particularly the constant traveling. However, I don't give much thought to changing my life style. I feel privileged because I'm doing what I want to do. It gives me a lot of pleasure and, I hope, others as well. It also gives me a vision of what I must pursue. So I will continue to play as long as I am able to do so.

John Browning

JOHN BROWNING

I III II III II III II III II III II III II III II I

So that he could eat breakfast and talk at the same time, John Browning chose the coffee shop at the Orrington Hotel in Evanston, Illinois, as the place for our interview. He was in town to teach a master class in piano at Northwestern University, a task he performs fifteen times a year despite a heavy schedule of one hundred or more concerts. Between sips of coffee, twelve cups of it, and puffs on his ever-present cigarette, he talked about his life as a concert pianist and about his views on the contemporary scene in classical pianism, especially as it related to the students he instructed.

I T'S hard to explain just what the students' focus is. On the one hand they seem to think that technique is everything, and on the other hand they lack the vitality and energy necessary to execute their wishes. The first task I have is to rid them of the "technique first" delusion. Somehow they have to be made to understand the importance of thinking in orchestral terms at the keyboard. A good pianist doesn't just play a melody, but plays a melody like a woodwind, or a string, or horn. This gives the music its color, the quality which so many young pianists lack and which is not associated per se with technique. All they bring to the piano is fingers. They haven't had their imaginations awakened to sound like Horowitz, for example, who can play ten voices and make them sound like ten different instruments. They just don't grasp that element of sound.

And as far as their technique is concerned, I'm not convinced that my students or any other American youngsters are that advanced. Of course I have to qualify that statement because I don't know from experience what the level of talent was fifty or sixty years ago. But my impression is that there hasn't been much improvement. The accounts of piano instruction at the St. Petersburg Conservatory or the Moscow Conservatory, particularly when the Lhevinnes were there, lead me to believe that the playing was far better than the playing at the Juilliard today. For one thing, the approach was much more distinct. They all revered Anton Rubinstein, so they followed his way of playing. Furthermore, the Russians have always started working with the students earlier. We begin so late; even in academic subjects we think youngsters can't learn a foreign language until they're eight or nine. Music especially should be started around the age of four or five.

So often the American students are not even remotely finished by the time they get to the university or conservatory, whereas in the Soviet Union most are ready by the time they're fifteen. By that time they have all the tools. There is really very little more to be done as far as approach and sound are concerned. Apparently, we do not have good enough teachers at the lower levels where it counts most. I think that the technical training in this country is spotty at best. Here you very rarely hear young pianists whose technique is truly finished. It may sound and look very impressive, but if you listen closely to their music, you'll hear a lot of flaws.

My conclusions are based on what I can observe while performing there on tour and what I can pick up by listening to their performances here. What I'd like to do is go to Russia for one or two weeks just to observe how their conservatories function. For all we know they may develop only those pianists who have a great deal of innate technique. Vladimir Ashkenazy, for example, I've been told, has said that he did not work very hard at developing his technique. Yet, from my observations, he seems to have put in a great deal of time on his technical skills and, for some reason, just doesn't want to talk about it. He does seem to have a perfectly natural facility in double thirds, double sixths, and other similar movements. He has an unusually small hand, but he does so many things easily and effortlessly that I'm inclined to believe he was born with a great amount of natural ability.

Of course the actual stance or position of the hands and fingers has much to do with the final effect of the performance. The Russian school, in imitation of Rubinstein, uses a higher bridge and a flatter finger than we do. The only variance is the Leschetizky school, which uses a very curved finger. As for me, I have no preference. When I play, I use anything that works. Half the time I'm not even aware of what I do. However, I believe very much in the correct use of strong weight in playing; I don't mean that one should attack the keyboard, but use strong weight which gives a much richer and less percussive sound than merely hitting the keys. The use of the wrist, too, is very important, but it's such an individual trait that no generalization about its use is valid. I've seen players who were too tight in the wrist and players who were too loose, but I can't really define the ideal or the norm.

In general, I just try to stay away from any kind of "method." Even as a child I avoided "methods" because I felt that, if I were going to be a fine pianist someday, I'd find my own way of getting there. As long as I played the piano as naturally as I could, I knew all the other facets of the art would fall into place. I always had a fairly natural technique; I always had a fairly natural sound at the keyboard, a sense of voicing, and I always was a natural pedaler, so I never even gave those things conscious attention. Yet, when I hear somebody who doesn't have the sound, I begin trying to figure out what's wrong. After the analysis comes the teaching. It's hard to say. A lot of things you yourself do, more or less naturally, you may have been taught but you can't remember. It's like remembering how you learned to read. I certainly can't remember. I was taught to read both words and music before I went to school. I was taught by my mother; I still don't know how and she doesn't remember. I'm not sure that anyone knows how we learn. Of one thing I am sure: Body size and weight determine to a great extent all of the other factors in piano technique, even hand stance and wrist flexibility.

Nonchalant as he was about his own technique, Browning had made more than a casual study of the techniques of others. In his opinion, had Arnold Schultz, author of Riddle of the Pianist's Finger, *been able fully to analyze and teach Vladimir Horowitz's technique, "he'd earn a million dollars." But the million dollars could not be realized because Schultz emphasized the wrong aspect of Horowitz's playing.*

It isn't Horowitz's technique; it is his sound. Schnabel had a certain kind of sound; Horowitz has a certain kind of sound. Technique isn't a matter of how quickly you can play the scales; it's the ability to produce many different sounds. *That* constitutes the highest ideal of technique.

The pedal plays an important part in voicing, too. Most of the young pianists today use the pedal as a crutch. Maybe it's because they've been brought up in the automobile age, but they use the pedal on a piano as an accelerator in a car. To use their phrase, they just "sit on it." They don't feel right unless the accelerator is constantly depressed. Consequently, you seldom hear a real legato. The playing is so notey that the new pianists cannot play a legato if they take the foot off the pedal. They were not trained to play in any other fashion. They use the pedal to cover up the sins they commit because of a void in their technical facility. When the pedal is used, it should be only for shading and for accent. But a pianist should not have to depend on it. That's one of the secrets of Horowitz's playing. He doesn't need to use the pedal and, when he does use it, he achieves very subtle shades and accents. The tricks he uses are fantastic. Yet he can play page after page of music without pedaling at all. Maybe that's why his use of pedal is so exciting: You know he doesn't have to use it because he voices so clearly and his lines are so strong. What I try to get through to the students is that, if they want to continue using as much pedal as they do, they'll have to sharpen their outlines or the pedal will make the music roar and confuse the ear.

The use of the sostenuto pedal depends more on individual preference. A certain amount of experimentation is necessary. When a virtuoso plays Bach, Mozart, Beethoven, or Schubert, he's not using the pianos they had. Even when he plays Chopin, he plays an instrument different from the one Chopin used. Hence the need for experimentation. I stick to the theory that, if it works, use it.

Certainly this advice isn't generally given to students. I spend almost no time at all on method, partly because I'm working with students who already have private teachers and I don't want to interfere with what they're being taught, and partly because there's insufficient time. If the physical aspect of their playing is very bad, there's very little that I can do to improve it in fifteen or twenty minutes. If it's good, I wouldn't want to change it anyway. Chiefly, I try to make them sound and voice conscious. That doesn't mean that I get immediate results, however. A few in the class will catch on and I can hear the change in their playing right away. But I know damn well they aren't going to remember much of what we did beyond eight hours after class. As for the rest of the students, the results may come as late as ten years after the classes. Something I've said or something they've done will lie in the subconscious and suddenly they hit upon it. And, best of all, they'll know it and then they'll make it part of themselves and become first-class pianists.

So far Browning had not mentioned the sort of music he asked his students to play and what sort of repertoire they should build for themselves. His selections comprised a mixture of the past and the present.

Anyone who hopes to be a concert pianist must still concern himself with understanding of style. George Szell put it pretty well when he said that nobody should consider himself a pianist if he can't play a Bach prelude and fugue without pedal. What most pianists today lack, as I mentioned before, is a real legato. Contrapuntal music from the Bach period trains pianists to follow linear voices and to phrase one voice against another. That's the formal phase of discipline in music. On the other hand, a pianist should loosen up a lot of classical music and tighten up a good deal of romantic music. Herein lies the freedom of music. So many artists feel that Mozart has to be played rigidly while Chopin can be performed as loosely as one wants. I think the exact opposite is true. A slow movement in Mozart should be played freely and expressively, whereas the rubatos in Chopin should be tightened.

In contemporary literature I'd certainly recommend Barber's Sonata because it seems it has gained a permanent position in the standard repertoire. His Concerto, too, is assuming its place. I've certainly premièred and played it often enough in concerts. And, of course, Prokofieff must be included. The avant garde literature hasn't arrived mainly, I think, because most of it just doesn't sound good on the piano. It's not written for the piano as a nineteenth-century romantic instrument. I shy away from such music myself. However, I certainly would recommend a certain amount of it for students. It is a part of our age.

I guess what I do recommend for students doesn't differ much from what I choose for myself, and a good number of my choices depend on like and dislike. I find, for example, that some works, like Brahms's Sonata in F Minor, come and go on my list of favorites. I fall in and out of love with works because I can play or hear one that I almost forgot about and suddenly see with fresh eyes and hear with new ears. That piece is then reinstated on the "love" list. Other works are perennial favorites, like Beethoven's Sonata, Opus 110, which I love to play anytime. The same holds true for most Chopin, especially the mazurkas and the Barcarolle, Opus 60. Bach's *Well-Tempered Clavier* is still the "Bible," but it isn't played as much for the public as it is for oneself. Bach's concerti, too, aren't all that successful in piano concerts because many of them, like the *Goldberg* Variations, sound better on the harpsichord and possibly are better reserved for that instrument. As for other concerti, I stick to the standards: Brahms, Beethoven, Mozart, Tchaikovsky, and Ravel. Another favorite of mine is Scriabin, especially his Third Sonata.

Two or three pieces of Liszt, for example the Sonata in B Minor (which I never learned), are wonderful pieces of music; but I play very little Liszt. Mine is a big technique, geared to producing large emotion. A Liszt Hungarian rhapsody doesn't always have much emotional or musical meaning, so technically it would be very difficult for me to play one. I'm not really interested in performing the Hungarian rhapsodies, so I just don't bother with them. Then, too, I'm not being pushed to learn new music all the time because a great deal of the learning of my repertoire was completed before I ever became a concert pianist. My teacher, Lee Pattison, saw to that. He made me memorize all the assigned music. Under him I memorized almost all the classical literature that I now play. The kids here at Northwestern are horrified when I tell them I had to play a newly memorized sonata every week. They're not used to that much work. Nevertheless, that was the discipline both Lhevinne and Pattison insisted on, and it paid off because, at the end of each year, I had memorized over fifty new works. I studied with Pattison for five years so, by the time I was twenty-one or twenty-two, most of the fundamental concert literature was in my musical storehouse. After that, I spent considerable time learning chamber music, which I also filed away in my memory for future use. Now, eighteen or nineteen years later, I'm still reaping the benefits of all that memorization.

Students often think there is some secret formula that the masters use to learn a work. If there is, I never found it. I simply play a piece over and over until I know it by heart. I don't have a photographic memory in the strict sense of the term, but if you ask about a specific passage in the score, I can tell you which page it's on. That doesn't mean, though, that I actually "see" the music as I play from memory. I suppose I just learn the sequences. For me, memorization is out and out hard work. If I decided to learn Scriabin's Sonata No. 3, for example, I might be able to do it in three days working ten hours a day. Of course, I wouldn't play it publicly right away. Music committed to memory should lie quietly for a while, simmering as it were, until it feels just right for performance. Memorizing is a personal process, and each pianist has to find the way that suits him best.

No system is perfect, either. Every performer fears memory slips. The best insurance against memory failure is practice, especially when preparing for an orchestral concert. Every artist is concerned with orchestra because, if anything goes wrong, it's difficult to know how to rectify it. Yet, we're all so used to playing without music, except for chamber music, that I think most artists would be even more nervous and uncomfortable using the score during the concert.

I never really made a decision when young to become a concert pianist. The atmosphere in which I was brought up influenced my growth into music, but I can't recall making any conscious decision about it. Both my parents were musicians and we had music in our house all the time, chamber music as well as every other kind. My dad played fiddle and mother, piano. I started studying with my mother when I was three and, by the time I was five, she thought I needed an outside teacher. When I was ten and eleven, I studied with the Lhevinnes for two summers in Denver. In a way, I simply grew with and into music, but I don't ever remember thinking that becoming a concert pianist was what I was going to do.

My mother never *made* me play the piano. It seemed to be the natural thing to do since music was part of our lives. But she did make me feel conscientious about work. Because both parents were excellent musicians, their critical standards were very high. We attended concerts together, and they made sure that I heard the best that was available; their judgments of what was good and what was bad were right on the button. All of this influenced my own development significantly since I was introduced to the best right from the beginning.

From the technical point of view, an early start is especially important. The kind of physical coordination you need for piano playing can't be begun too soon. In that respect, playing an instrument is like learning to be a figure skater; if you're not pretty damn good by age sixteen, you can forget figure skating competition. It's one of the paradoxes in American life that I don't understand. We are so sports oriented that we never question the fact that we start out kids in swimming or skating at the age of three or four, but we delay the forming of artistic talent until it's almost too late. True, we've instituted the Suzuki violin method, and I confess I don't know much about it. But the fact that it apparently works for a large number of

John Browning conducting a master class at Northwestern University. *Rich Sato, Northeastern Illinois University Photo Department*

people means that it must have shortcuts, and that alone makes it highly suspicious to me.

On the other hand, there's no guarantee that an early start, discipline, and parental involvement will make a performer successful. Some artists have a meteoric rise for a while; they become a public fad because of a flashy repertoire or some new kind of showy technique, but there's no substance to their art. In the long run, the standard stuff, both in quantity and in quality, does win out. Also, winning prizes in competition helps. Right after I went to Juilliard, I won three prizes which in and of themselves weren't critical, but they made the public and the critics aware of me. At least I had been noticed. The value of exposure can't be underestimated. In 1965, I performed with George Szell (I'm a Szell addict) on a twelve-week-long State Department tour. We hit all the big capitals of Western Europe, as well as Russia and the Iron Curtain countries. It was a very special tour for me because, after that, I seemed to be on my way. Finally, I'd add the element of growth. It's part of that solid stuff I spoke of. Through growth you make yourself constantly interesting to hear. Without growth, any career is in trouble.

His philosophy of growth applied to music, too. In fact, he and Leonard Bernstein had had long discussions on the present and future state of music and neither had come to any solid conclusions. Browning reluctantly admitted that we may find now a situation where music may not be written at all.

It's possible we've come to an end. And what happens then? It's like anything else. It starts getting lost. We in the concert field have been like custodians in a museum: We play music, but we don't create. The bulk of the repertoire we play is music of the past, so we're really just curators. We preserve, but we're not doing much original composition. In the past sixty years, very little new stuff has gone into the permanent record file compared to what was produced in previous eras. There might be something permanent in the vast amount of avant garde music that has been written, but concert artists generally are just not interested in performing such work. It was written by people who specialized in it, not people who had careers in the open market to think of. Sam Barber and I very often go to a concert with some avant garde music in it, and I know he is far more tolerant of it than I am. Yet, as soon as we leave the hall, he takes the words right out of my mouth: "Gee, it would be nice to hear a good tune, wouldn't it?" I find my own reaction to it is very much that of the layman. I want to be able to take something out of the hall, and I don't always. Often the performance is over before I realize it, and I don't remember anything. I don't remember line, I don't remember harmony, I don't remember voices, and I don't remember anything else. Maybe that's my fault. Here again this whole business of judging music is difficult because we keep forgetting how much junk was written in the past which we have blessedly forgotten long ago. Maybe, if we add up all the serious music that was written, say between 1920 and 1977, and find it far more impressive in the future than it now appears, it will be because we hear so much junk that it's hard to separate the wheat from the chaff in the period in which the music is played and heard.

And the future of concert halls is as tenuous as the future of music making. The arts are getting incredibly expensive. Deficits are just skyrocketing. The private sources are drying up. The government is not yet helping with anywhere near the kind of money that is needed, and survival may end up being a matter of dollars and cents more than anything else. It very easily could be that we cannot support the kind of culture we've had. And it depends on the public, too. Obviously, if the public stops going to concerts, then concerts will stop. That's something we can't foretell for sure. Public concerts as we think of them really are relatively new—about 100 or 125 years old—so there is still time for growth.

Another thing that has to be faced: So many of the concert halls are now located in bad neighborhoods. Symphony Hall in Boston is not in a good area, nor is the Academy of Music in Philadelphia. Unless cities start cleaning up the areas around the present facilities, the concert halls are going to have to be rebuilt in better neighborhoods. What happens to the inner cities definitely has some effect on the future of concerts.

Browning is also worried about the future of concert pianists in America, especially in the area of rising stars.

There are not very many Americans, which is disturbing. So many of the pianists and teachers who came out of the Lhevinne studio and similar schools of foreign influence are dead now. Americans are being taught by Americans most of the time and, since we are a somewhat new entry into the concert field, we are creating inbreeding. There hasn't been enough impressively trained young talent emerging from this country. An awful lot of the young artists going places are either in Russia or Europe. I think Russia is doing the best job in turning out students.

The doubt and uncertainty that he expressed concerning the future of music generally in the United States creeps into his discussion of his own future. He doubts that he will ever go into private teaching because of his travel schedule. Nor is he interested in conducting.

I've seen too many good instrumentalists turn into lousy conductors and I just don't want any part of it. It must be very exciting to stand up there and not have to worry about whether you are in top technical shape and still have all the sound come out. I just don't think that temperamentally it would be suitable for me. As to the teaching, I certainly didn't seek any of it, but it has its compensations. It takes very little time out of the year, and I enjoy it because the one thing it forces me to do is to reevaluate constantly. If you tell the students something, you've got to be pretty sure you're right. You have to be articulate and you have to say it in such a way that it won't be misunderstood. But I never expected to be a teacher. I just fell into it when I was asked to do a few classes at Tanglewood, then at Kent State, and then at Ravinia. They all seemed to go well, so I've stuck with it.

Since music is his whole life, Browning pays close attention both to his predecessors and his contemporaries, and has definite opinions of those he considers great. Lhevinne was an "extraordinary talent."

Rachmaninoff, Dame Myra Hess, and Solomon rank as "wonderful and satisfying." Artur Schnabel is revered: "He is a great god for me." Two others receive special mention.

Rubinstein usually plays marvelously. When he's off, he plays badly; but when he's on, his performances are fantastic. Horowitz has always staggered me in many ways, although I don't like everything he does. He's probably the finest Scriabin player I've ever heard, and his Scarlatti is also excellent. I'm the least happy with some of his Chopin which I find, oddly enough, getting a little bit mannered sometimes. In fact, a musician friend of mine in New York commented that Horowitz very often could take a very structured piece like a Beethoven sonata or a Chopin nocturne and distort it, and yet could take a very floundering form like a Scriabin sonata and play it tight as a drum. I concur with him in that observation, but I have such respect for Horowitz that, even if he does something that might set my teeth on edge, I just ignore it because I'm positive that there will be something in the performance that will completely dazzle me.

As far as my own playing is concerned, I think it has changed. It's gotten warmer, not really because I have tried harder, but because I think I know a lot more than I did. The older one becomes, the more the body begins to wear down, and that's when the real intensity and integrity and warmth of the spirit come out. It's almost as if some supernatural or preternatural power compensates for the loss of youth. I'm very much a believer in the adage that God helps those who help themselves; yet, if I've played extraordinarily well, I somehow get the feeling that I've not done it alone. Despite the fact that I work very hard and practice a great deal, I've had this peculiar feeling of gratitude to whatever it was that intervened. I have no other way of describing it or of knowing it, but occasionally I feel it.

The layman, the audience, seems to see a lot of glamor and fascination in our way of life that we don't see. In reality, we're just slave labor; we go to a hall and practice; then we rest, eat, and dress for the concert. We play the concert, go to an after-theater party, retire for a few hours sleep, then catch a morning plane to the next stop. It becomes very routine, very boring. If the artist doesn't change in some way, the boredom will appear in the playing no matter how he tries to hide it. The change for me has been in the warmth.

That doesn't mean that I'm satisfied with every performance. There are times when I wish that I had played this concert better, or that work differently; but, generally speaking, I have no regrets. Even as I reminisce about my past, I see how in some respects, both in terms of music and in terms of piano playing, I did things backwards. I had a Schnabel teacher [Pattison] when I probably should have had another kind, and I worked on advanced repertoire when I should have done more simple stuff; but it has all paid off in the long run. I play the piano as well as I can; I make music as well as I can.

On the other hand, no performing artist is ever in complete control over a situation, either. I think stage fright plays some part in the final product. Every performance has some of that, although the exact nature of it is difficult to pin down. It begins to build in the morning and reaches a climax by mid-afternoon. That's when it's worst. I don't have bad nerves, but I often wake up with a tight knot in the stomach which gets tighter as the day progresses. Locale and program seem to have little to do with it. I can be as calm as a quiet sea for a New York concert, but nervous as a cat for a performance in a small town. The reverse is equally true. So there's no way to prepare for it or avoid it.

Audiences, too, have their effect on one's playing. I can sense that the communication isn't going well, but I don't know whether I'm not playing well or the audience is not responsive. Then there are times when the whole thing is a total disaster; you play a rotten piano, in a lousy hall, with a flat audience. It can really get to you.

The last cigarette in the pack was lit; the waitress served Browning's twelfth cup of coffee. His eyes flickered for an instant, possibly to show that he had not been completely satisfied with his journey into himself. He confessed that his values had not quite stabilized. He wanted to leave a legacy of certain values which he considered important, but which had not yet crystallized in his own mind. Interestingly enough, these values would not come from his playing, but from his teaching and his "hearing." Whether or not he would be able to evaluate his legacy from beyond the grave was questionable.

I doubt very much whether there is any life beyond this one. I think the hereafter is probably one big sleep. Again, I tend to be very pragmatic about such things. So, if there's going to be a life after death, fine; if there isn't, fine—as long as they don't have a bunch of harps playing up there! I love them in an orchestra, but I think I would get very irritated if I had to hear thirty-five harps playing all at once.

Alicia de Larrocha

ALICIA DE LARROCHA

The small room at the Salisbury Hotel in Manhattan must have seemed confining to a concert pianist who owns two homes in Spain, but it in no way diminished the graciousness of Alicia de Larrocha as she invited me to a chair opposite her. All earlier attempts with her management to arrange an appointment had failed because her schedule was so heavily booked with concert and recording engagements.

A personal phone call to New York before her Ravinia concert resulted in receiving an invitation to meet her after the performance to discuss the matter. She had finished her performance of the Chopin F Minor Concerto, and we met backstage. Unfortunately, our conversation was just getting started when the lights dimmed to announce the end of the evening. She indicated that she would have several hours free on Sunday morning in New York before she left on a tour through Mexico and South America. So now we were ready to get to serious matters.

Mme. de Larrocha is not too keen on giving interviews because she sometimes finds it difficult to express her complete views on music in English. However, she underestimates herself, especially when with a quiet smile and soft voice she narrates the story of her beginnings in music.

IT seems to me that I was born listening to music because I was completely surrounded by it. Both my mother and my aunt had been students of Enrique Granados, but my mother abandoned her piano studies when she married. Not so my aunt. She played and she taught piano, too, so I had a strong musical environment. My first toy was my aunt's piano, which I much preferred to dolls. She finally decided that the one-year-old had ruined it enough, so she locked it. I had a nasty temper, and to show my displeasure at losing my toy, I started to scream and beat my head on the tile floor until it bled. To quiet me, my aunt promised that if I behaved myself, she would allow me to take up the piano seriously. So when I was two, she tutored me, giving me a little at a time. During this time, my aunt had been teaching at the Marshall Academy, so one day she decided to take me to hear a small recital given by the children attending the school.

When the recital ended, I grabbed Mr. Marshall by the trouser leg and told him that I was there and wanted to play the piano. He laughed and said that I was too young. All I could think of was that everyone seemed against me and that just made me more determined to learn how to play the piano. I think now that if they had given in easily, I might have changed my mind. Maybe it's an inborn trait, but we Spanish sometimes seem to love opposition. If you say, "Yes," I'll say, "No," just to be contrary. At any rate, Mr. Marshall finally relented, probably more out of curiosity than for any other reason. He let me play for him, but what I knew I had picked up listening to my aunt's students, so I consequently played everything by ear. He became more curious when I started to improvise and decided to give me lessons. However, there seemed to be no steadfast method to his teaching. He was frequently critical, but he let me do pretty much what I wanted, now and then substituting what he thought would do me more good. And so at a very young age, music became my life, though I confess I never thought about giving concerts or making music my career. I just wanted music to be as much a part of my physiology as the heart, lungs, and other vital organs were. Music fulfilled a need, a craving, and that was it.

Even in my early teens, though I continued my lessons, I had no plans for a career. Once in a while, some organization or ladies' group would ask me to play here or there, and I did. My teacher allowed me to play publicly two or three times a year, but I never prepared for a concert in excellence. I played programs for experience, but never to really show how I excelled at the keyboard. Then I had an opportunity to play with an orchestra. Fernandos Arbos, the conductor, knew me and asked me to play a Mozart concerto. Well, we did the concerto together, and that was the end of it. The revolution came, my teachers all left Spain, and for three years I did nothing but play for myself and write a little music, again only for myself.

When the revolution was over, my teachers returned and we started over again. But still there was no definite career. Now and then I was invited to play in Paris or Switzerland, but it was all on a catch-as-catch-can basis. When I was invited, I went; when there were no invitations, I stayed home. I didn't know whether I was really building any reputation or not. My parents were noncommittal about the whole thing. They appreciated my sensitivity, but never pushed me to play the piano. If I wanted to play, they let me play; and if I didn't choose to play, they kept quiet about it. In this regard, they were both intelligent and clever in allowing me to find out things for myself. At times my mother almost seemed terrified at the thought of my living the life of a pianist. She told me to live now, while I was young. Her main concern was that I was spending too much time at the piano. She was afraid that I would become ill, so she told me to get more fresh air, to go for walks, and to visit the mountains. It was difficult to convince her that I played because I wanted to and because it gave me great pleasure. I suppose it did seem somewhat odd to them because neither of my two sisters or brother took an avid interest in playing the piano. Also I didn't appear at the time to be going anywhere because all I did was play an occasional recital when I was asked.

Then in 1954, I was invited to play a concert with the Los Angeles Philharmonic Orchestra. I had been invited to appear as soloist by Alfred Wallenstein, the conductor, but I didn't take it too seriously. I didn't know if it would really happen or not. Yet in a month I received a contract, so I came and played. Then again a lot of nothing. But in 1965, Herbert Breslin, head of a concert management in New York, wrote that he had heard my records and wanted me to come to New York. By now I had been married five years, and my husband thought that perhaps Breslin wanted money to start a promotion and publicity campaign, so we never answered the letter. A few months later, Breslin wrote again and my husband said, "I see you have received another letter from the man with the trumpet." You understand, Mr. Breslin uses a trumpet logo on his stationery. Well, he wrote again for the third time, telling me he could arrange for me to play five concerts with the New York Philharmonic Orchestra. That letter I answered, even though my manager in Madrid thought I shouldn't. But that was the real start of my career and it was like a mountain falling on me. After that, everything just fell into place.

In an era when concert pianists frequently obtain their recognition via the competition route, Mme. de Larrocha's success is all the more remarkable. She does not, however, regret that she was not a participant. In fact she's not in sympathy with the entire procedure.

I think the whole system is wrong, completely wrong. It has nothing to do with music or the artist. It's like an Olympic which is artificial and mechanical. It's just work, work, work to make the competition, but then what? If the pianists are any good, they don't need a competition. Besides, if they do win, they merely receive a prize and a series of concerts which sometimes turns the pianists into mere machines. That isn't music, nor is it art. Great publicity has about the same effect. It gets you a name and a lot of public notice, but whether you're a good musician or not doesn't count for much. I'm sure there are many artists who can't build successful careers because no one is encouraging or pushing them along the way. I'll admit that chance plays some part in the success of pianists, but if there's no one behind the artist, keeping him in the public eye, his chances are likewise slim. Still, I surely am not the one to ask about building a career because I don't know any sure method. For me it was simply the force of love for music, something that I had to do because music was such an integral part of my life. I never planned a future and I

Alicia de Larrocha with her only teacher, Frank Marshall

still don't. My husband and my manager take care of the concerts and programs I play. If I don't like a suggested program, I indicate my preferences and then we make the necessary changes. Nor am I legacy conscious. As I told you, I might be considered as primarily a rather selfish pianist because I play for myself. And when I'm gone, my only wish is that people have had some enjoyment from my work and they won't think I was too nasty as a person! I don't look back, either. It would be a joy to meet Beethoven, Bach, and Schumann because they were such great artists, but I don't spend much time dreaming about it. I have a tendency to be moody at times. If it suits my mood to wish to have lived in the past, it is my way of escaping, nothing more. Of course I try never to let my moodiness interfere with my playing, but it has happened occasionally. I might be geared to play well when suddenly the piano sounds as if I'm striking the keys too hard and then I begin to play badly. It is the most miserable feeling I know, and the only way out of it is to become completely involved in the music. The music will carry me through. However, I can never predict what will happen during a performance. If I try to talk myself into being more calm, I start getting nervous; and if I begin with a case of nerves and just go out and play, I enjoy the concert and it seems to come off well. It's the story of my life. It has always been unpredictable with a good measure of improvisation thrown in. In fact, I have enjoyed my life being this way.

Learning new repertoire has become more difficult for Mme. de Larrocha because of numerous infringements on her time. However, she doesn't change her own individual method which accents the importance of fingering.

First of all, I'm not the kind of person who likes to sit down to a score and play it from beginning to end. I study the music carefully first to form an idea of what it is all about. Then I seek passages or sections which offer the most difficulty, especially in regard to fingering. For me, the fingering is very important. I may decide on using a certain finger to produce a particular tone, but if it doesn't work, then I have to change the fingering accordingly. That's why I don't advocate practicing away from the piano as some pianists do; a decision on fingering may not be practical at the concert hall, and by that time it's a little late to change. It's better to have a practical fingering worked out ahead of time, especially for me because fingering is the base of security, I think. Sometimes, too, I have to play a piece very slowly to solidify the memorization of the part. Slowness also helps to check note accuracy and phrasing, because when you play in slow motion, just as in viewing a movie run slowly, you see every detail and at the same time reinforce the memory. You are able to see chords more clearly, the form, the design, the harmonic groupings, and so on. It helps enormously to know the phrases, the ritardandos, an accent here, an accent there, an ending phrase, a starting phrase, that is, all the details.

This memorization of the rhythmical accents in every phrase is a very important memory aid, but not quite as reliable as the memorizing of the phrases, cadences, and form. I don't believe much in vision memory. It seems unsure and leaves me feeling rather insecure. Also I don't practice above the keys, omitting the aural aspect, that is. I may do this on occasion when I'm afraid I'll disturb someone, but it seems too unnatural. Then, too, the fingers need much work. When I was learning to play, my teacher tailored exercises for me. Besides the usual scales and chords, he measured my fingers and like a doctor prescribed exercises that were good for *me*. He realized that a student had to work within his limits, so what he devised didn't go beyond my bounds. I had to open up my hands and play slowly. By staying on a chord, I could feel the stretch. I wish I had a naturally wider expanse, but I don't. I wouldn't care for longer fingers, just a broader hand spread. But by training and hard work I've managed to overcome that limitation.

I'm also told that I keep my fingers very close to the keyboard. Well, that's my system. It doesn't mean that it will work for everyone. I obtain the results I want doing it that way, and that's what counts. Systems change, too. The instruments I learned to play were different from what I'm playing now, so I've had to adapt. The new pianos have a different action as well as a different tone. If it means more curvature of the fingers to obtain the particular tone I want, I do

it; if less curvature is needed, I use less. The same holds true for pedaling. If there's too much sound or too much reverberation, I will use
less pedal. If the sound seems dry and the acoustics are dry, I use
more pedal because I need the singing sound. In the long run, I
believe an artist trusts his instincts about systems and methods. But if
some physical qualities tend to be limited, then the artist has to com-
pensate for them. Small hands, for instance, have great difficulty in
spanning large stretches. As I mentioned, exercises which stretch the
hand are helpful. However, by using your musical imagination in
pedaling, phrasing, and so forth, you can still produce the big sound
and overcome the technical problem. Still, I continue to do stretching
exercises, even if I have to use one hand to help stretch the fingers of
the other.

*When asked if she considered herself a specialist of any sort, her
reply was in the negative.*

I'm not engaged in any special period and I've never really wanted to
be considered a specialist in anything. I was musically educated in all
the contemporaries, but in a traditional way. I didn't go beyond
Prokofieff. It would be impossible for me to single out one or two
composers as favorites or preferences. In my choice of composers, I
enjoy going from one to the other. I suppose I might be called a free
spirit in this regard. I totally believe that in every period there are
new moods, new idioms, and people are searching for new systems. I
know we can't stand still, but I'm not much involved in the so-called
new music so I take a wait-and-see attitude. My feeling is that hu-
manity today has gone a bit crazy to some extent and everything,
including music, has gotten out of control. So we will have to return
to the very real, the very sensitive music as well as a sensible way of
life. We are going to have to make a complete return to sensibility. I
don't know this for sure, of course; it's only a feeling I have. I don't
want to put this on a comparative basis, either. We can't possibly
compare the artists of today with men like Liszt and Anton Rubinstein. The piano is different, the tastes of the audience are different,
and the possibilities certainly aren't the same. We think and feel dif-

ferently, too, because customs and priorities have changed. Every period of music history has shown different tastes, manners, and techniques. In any era there was a group of excelling artists who worked at the highest level until little by little new styles and manners eroded their positions and new great artists replaced them. But no replacement ever diminished the greatness of the true artists. Unfortunately, we don't have recordings of our predecessors, so we really don't know how they played. We only have the written testimony from those individuals that heard them in concert. I rather suspect that audiences today might be somewhat disappointed if they heard some of these famous virtuosos of the past in concert now because they would judge the music in the light of their present-day tastes and preferences.

We hear that the Romantic period, for instance, was the period of virtuosity, of emphasis on technique. But we don't know what they meant by technique. If we mean sheer mechanics, then we must judge solely on the basis of the instrument of that time. The pianos of Liszt and Chopin were so light to the touch that just blowing on the keys would almost produce the sound. Then again, the sound was smaller, and that's how it should have been because the concert halls accommodated only several hundred people, and many recitals were given in private homes or fashionable salons. But if Liszt and Chopin had to play on a modern piano, no one knows how they would fare.

Beyond the mere mechanics, you have the real meaning of technique. It is sound, interpretation, tone, and musical line. It is phrasing, accent, melody, and musical conception. In general, technique in the mechanical sense will do nothing for you. You must see what technique you must apply at this moment in this particular piece you are playing. But it must always be natural, not forced. In the romantic composers, for example, the phrases are long thus giving much feeling to the work. In the classical composers, the law of musical form is more obvious and must be adhered to. But whatever the artist does with the music must ultimately come from his musical conception. I have my concepts, others have theirs; and they shouldn't be compared. After all, music is music. I play music not because I want to be compared, but because I love it.

Misha Dichter and his wife Cipa, who often practice and perform together

MISHA DICHTER

I III II III II III II III II III II III II III II III II III II I

My parents didn't really encourage or guide me along the route to becoming a concert pianist. They wanted me to become a doctor. I listened to them up to a point, but at age fifteen I decided to become a concert pianist.

Thus Misha Dichter began the recollections of his life as a piano virtuoso who, at age thirty-four, has achieved a degree of success seldom attained by many at a much later stage of their careers. Hours of practice, a strong belief in self, and a fair amount of luck combined to bring him to this pinnacle.

Once I made my decision, I began practicing for long periods, sometimes as much as twelve hours a day. And instead of working on formal exercises, such as Czerny or Clementi, I spent one solid year practicing various standard exercises such as scales, arpeggios, trills, and so forth just to develop my technique. Now I practice less—about four hours a day when I'm traveling; but when I'm learning new repertoire during the summer, I'm usually able to fit in six hours of daily practice.

Of course, during those formative years I studied with numerous teachers, especially in California when I was a youngster. The most important of these was Aube Tzerko, a former Schnabel pupil. Then, after moving to New York, I continued my studies with Madame Rosina Lhevinne at Juilliard. I was eighteen when I began my studies with her.

Most of all I remember the belief I had in myself. I see now that success is a combination of destiny, luck, and hard work; but in those days, when my career was beginning, I was too young even to consider that it might not work. I knew from my teens that I wanted to be a concert pianist, although I had no concept of all that was included in my choice. I think there was some sort of inner consciousness that knew that something was there even though I had a great deal to accomplish pianistically; but there was still a blind belief in myself and in my abilities. It was the Moscow Tchaikovsky Prize in 1966 that launched my career. I was twenty years old at the time, and the ensuing whirlwind didn't give me any time to think about the future. I'm sure most people in other fields who plan a career have time to sit back and view their prospects at age thirty, especially if nothing big has come their way yet. I didn't have a chance to do that. Besides, I'm convinced that for an instrumentalist, if nothing has happened by age thirty, it probably won't happen anyway.

I consider my first ten years experimental; I went to places rather unknown to me. But now I know exactly where I want to go, both geographically and artistically. There are no uncharted places that I still have to go to perform. In those first ten years, for instance, I toured South America, but I'm not interested in playing there anymore. I'll take a vacation there, but that's the extent of it. I want to divide my time between the States and Europe, with an occasional side trip to Japan and Israel.

Artistically, besides keeping up with concerts and repertoire, I have a little bit of the conducting bug in me primarily because there are so many bad conductors around. I think the world could use more good conductors, but I don't have the time for that right now. However, it is in the future. I can't say the same for composing, though. I once took composition very seriously but have now limited it to composing cadenzas for Mozart concerti.

Then there is teaching. Right now I confine myself to one or two master classes in Aspen during the summer and maybe one or two similar classes during the winter months for one or two weeks. Since I spend my summers in Aspen anyway, I can fit in the master classes without too much inconvenience, but my schedule is generally too heavy to allow for much more. Right now, too, I'm gobbling up vast amounts of chamber music that were virtually unknown to me. Just in the past ten days I've been working on Schubert's A Major Violin and Piano Duo, Brahms's C Major Trio, a Mozart trio, the Schubert B-flat Trio, the Mozart B-flat Violin Sonata, the Beethoven F Major Cello Sonata, and the Rachmaninoff Cello Sonata. This last work alone has taken up endless hours of work. After all, the music comes first. ·

In addition, I take a rather dim view of the master class format. I find it rather confusing in some respects. Primarily, I have no way of knowing whether what I have to offer comes across to the students in that kind of surrounding. I have noticed that this format of teaching is often simply an ego trip for the pianist conducting the class. I would much rather give private lessons to very talented students. In fact, private teaching is very much in my future plans. I would like to take on talented students and see how far along I could bring them. I've developed many techniques in my playing over the last few years, and I feel that I can offer some definite ideas that will help young pianists, especially in the area of memorization. I've devised what I call my "system," which I believe anyone can learn; and since memory, or rather fear of the loss of it, is a major factor in a performer's stage fright, I think I can give him confidence in that area.

On a larger scale, I break down the form of the piece into its larger structural sections. In the smallest possible sense, I memorize intervallic relationships and harmonic blocks that are common throughout the entire movement of the complete piece. If the piece is based, for instance, on the interval of the sixth, then that interval will permeate the entire movement and form harmonic units. And whenever it crops up it not only contributes to an understanding of the piece, but offers a way to memorize it. Thus, I memorize harmonic structures which are related to intervallic structure so that, when I come to fixed points of harmony, I am not memorizing senseless details but rather blocks of harmonic sound along with all the secondary units surrounding that vital point. So even if I lose some details in that first couple of days of work, my mind remains fixed on those big blocks and I have a picture not only of the harmony, but also of harmonic structure or melodic pattern, because by then the hand has formed almost a visual image of those blocks and I have a picture not only of the harmony, but the hand relative to these main blocks.

There is, however, a kind of "learning" that takes place before the breaking down is undertaken. I play through a complete work a few times, even badly if it's a difficult piece, to give me an idea of the overall shape of it. Then, if it's a technically problematic piece, I'll single out the places that are the most awkward technically and I'll work on these as intensely as possible so that they become as easy as any other part of the piece. Consequently, they become second nature to me as I look at the overall structure of the piece. I'll make a daily exercise of a given passage if it's really a stickler. I can also memorize a work rather quickly when I have to. It's not a matter of talent. I devised this system for myself several years ago so that, if I really have to memorize something in a hurry, I can sit down and after four or five hours of intense study and a terrific headache, I have the piece memorized. I won't say that I can in four or five hours memorize a concerto that I've never played before, but anything I learn of the piece that day, even though it's my first acquaintance with it, will be memorized; and if it's not, then I know that I haven't really studied it.

The problem students have with this approach is, in a nut shell, seeing the leaves without the trees; they have no concept of the structure of the composition and do not understand how to look at a piece as a conductor would without having the problems of playing the instrument itself. They get so involved in the problems of the piano, which I confess are many, that they really lose sight of the fact that this phrase goes with that phrase, and that all the phrases add up to this entire movement or that entire section. There isn't a sense of architecture. The pianist must think orchestrally. I don't know that that's propagated by any given school of playing, but whenever I'm learning a piece or thinking about the ultimate sound of the work, I like to orchestrate it in my mind. The piano is a rather monotonous sounding instrument if you don't try to vary the textures in the voices.

In my own playing, I use low wrists and round curved fingers. That's the way I was taught, and now I don't even consciously think about it. My hand just goes that way. And as the years go by, I notice my wrists are getting lower and lower because I realize that's what good accuracy is all about—never even leaving the key. Arm weight comes into the picture, too, especially when I'm playing chords. It's necessary for a big sound that's not harsh to have the sound come from the shoulder and the whole arm. Some of this results from my changing the height of the bench. I used to sit very low about three years ago. Now I've raised the bench. I don't know that it makes a big difference, but it feels better.

You see, I'm constantly learning. Even in the last four or five months I've made adjustments in my style. There is this matter of getting the wrists lower, and now I am beginning to flatten the fingers a bit for closeness. And I think there's a greater precision now that recording again has forced me to listen better to my own playing. Initially, all the things that sounded fine in the practice room sounded quite different in the play-backs; this caused me to rethink many things and has been a very rewarding learning process.

Incidentally, all this talk of hand, wrist, arm, and so on isn't meant as a directive for teaching young children to play the piano. Children have to be introduced to music long before they play. At home we played various albums of Bach, Haydn, Mozart, and others when our two children were little as a way of introducing them to music. In teaching a child, I wouldn't start him at the keyboard, but instead *away* from it. I believe that music structure should come first and should be developed through listening experiences. After he has been shown something of the beauty of the music, then he can approach an instrument.

Regarding the forced separations of my being on tour, my wife Cipa and I agree. They are very healthy. People who have what can be considered normal jobs, going to offices every day, coming home regularly, having weekends together, and then going on the same holidays together, tend to take each other for granted. With us, being

Misha Dichter with his wife Cipa and their two children, Gabriel and Alexander

together is still a special occasion. On the other hand, when my wife and I tour together and perform together, our children rarely accompany us because of their schooling.

Sandwiched between all his feverish activity relative to his concerts and teaching, are sets of tennis at which he claims to be "pretty good." He also admits to being a "movie and theater buff." But formal vacations seem always to be connected with his profession.

This is supposed to be my free time now during August, and here we are backstage at Ravinia. This summer has been something really crazy. I try to have something that resembles a vacation at the very end of August for about ten days, at which time I'll be worrying about what program I have to get together for the fall season.

If you start worrying about upcoming concerts during your "free time," you must really get nervous before the concerts themselves.

I used to be nervous before concerts, but I thought there must be a way to calm this sort of feeling beforehand. I discovered that, if I was to play chamber music and I knew that there would be a score on the piano, I'd be much calmer; so I thought, "If the only thing you're going to be worried about is memory, let's find some system." So I devised the system we spoke of earlier and so far it's worked very well.

Possible memory failure is certainly an unpleasant thought and I'm sure there's not one of us who would say that he or she had always played spotless performances and had never forgotten anything. There's always somebody who's had some bad experience at one point or another. But if the artist is as perfectly prepared as possible with a complete understanding of the harmony and relationship of parts, and if the artist is rested and reasonably relaxed, and then still forgets something, then he's human, thank goodness! No mind can work like a constantly accurate computer, and there has to be a moment when it just turns off for a second. One can't concentrate every second in a two-hour program. Sometimes, too, there will be an off day, maybe because of a slight illness or the nature of the program; all this will have its effect.

Then again my mind used to play games with me during a performance. I would think, "Where will you forget this time?" and, of course, I *would* forget. Naturally! I was waiting for it, and it arrived. If it was a small lapse, my mind was pleased; if a big one, it was even more pleased! I had to learn to turn this off by having the positive impulses to keep going and not even allowing that devil to work. The concentration has to be not on the memory, but on the structure at hand. "I'm in this key, I'm following the alto line here leading to that soprano line there." If you're thinking of those things, you won't have a chance to ask, "What if I forget!"

When I'm on stage and working at my best, I'm three or four seconds ahead of what's going on at each second. And so that if it gets down to two seconds, or one second ahead, I'm still ahead of it and I still know what I'm doing. If the fingers are going without the mental process, they are actually ahead of the pursuit. It's all probably related to the time interval between the stimulus of the brain wave and the action itself.

Feelings of depression and incompetency, though, are as common in artists as they are in anyone else. I used to have more periods than now of saying, "I really can't play at all." I learned to slow up the thought process completely. If I started playing and I thought it didn't sound good, and it felt terrible, I began playing slower and slower until I'd be playing a note every second, for example, until I understood that my hand hadn't strayed from the music. What happens is that the mind isn't thinking quite of the harmonies or the melodic impulses fast enough to dictate to the muscle.

I've never looked upon my performances as a job to be done, but there certainly have been days when I felt like forgetting the whole thing and not going to the concert. There were times when I thought all the elements involved in a concert were against me: the likely possibility of a bad conductor, bad orchestra, lousy hall, bad instruments, and a program I'm not very interested in. Then I'll wake up in the morning and say, "I'll just have to get through it somehow."

It is most important to develop an attitude of confidence about performing. There are all sorts of details about pedaling, the Russian school of ten levels of pedaling, hands close to the keys, and different ways of playing octaves and chords; but I think none of these are as important as the basic attitude that, if you prepare for a concert, look forward to it.

Concerning conductors, there's a large group that I've had most pleasurable relationships with. At the top of my list is Giulini. Then there might be several others. I remember a very exciting weekend of Tchaikovsky concerti with Bernstein. It's hard to single out people. Everyone is special in some way of performing. Some are easier to get along with than others. A few of the older, well-known conductors, who will remain nameless, are quite set in their ways and those experiences I take as learning experiences. They have their ideas about the piece and I, for the time being, fit my playing into that mold for the sake of peace. With my contemporaries, however, I have fun arguing about the differences in approach and rendition, and the open-mindedness of these sessions often brings out the best in both parties, and the consequence is a good performance.

As colleagues, we pianists really don't bother to criticize each other very much; we leave that to the idiot reviewers. We're fortunate in that our musician friends are very positive in their approach to things. Then, too, we've made a point of avoiding people who might be in any way jealous or envious. There may be a little nit-picking about incidentals in a performance but, generally speaking for myself and my wife, nothing makes us happier than a terrific piano performance. If it's honest and it comes off wonderfully for somebody else, we're as happy as can be.

As for special composers out of the past, my choice would have to be Robert Schumann, because I think he was the twentieth-century man. He was certainly ahead of his time. Compositionally, rhythmically, melodically, and harmonically, he was absolutely ahead and I think people of his period were suspicious that maybe he was a little too crazy and experimental. Of all the composers of the past, Schumann fascinates me the most.

But I wouldn't want to move back to his time. I don't crave that at all; I prefer the present because of the reality of the recording age that we live in. I can't imagine what it would have been like a hundred years ago to have played a concert and realize that that's the end of it. An artist might think he had played well, but would have no way of checking his reaction. He could continually be deceiving himself because he could not criticize his own work. The same would hold true if he thought he had not played well. The recording would be the evidence. There's something marvelous about being able to hear yourself and study from your own mistakes, from your own performances, and to hear and to study others on records as well.

A great regret of mine is that recital series are no longer flourishing in this country. One by one they are folding. Maybe the reason is that there isn't a grass-roots love of music here. It seems that people go to the symphony because it's just the thing to do. I'm a skeptic about these things. I'm even more pessimistic about the future. The opera and the symphony perhaps will become more of a social event than a recital or a chamber concert, which is considered by many at the bottom of social musical forum. I love chamber music the most now. And before that my preference was playing a Mozart concerto with a terrific chamber orchestra. Playing chamber music is like a new life for me.

In Europe, there's more seriousness about music. Children are brought up on classical music; it's more evident around the home.

The rain continued relentlessly. The orchestra outside began tuning up as if to signal the end of our brief chat. I wondered aloud what Dichter thought would happen to all his efforts, his energy, his talent.

I consider myself lucky in that I'm so involved with my work that it gives me pleasure just to play, and I don't think of myself as a caretaker of some spirit that's going to go bouncing along. I'm happy that I'm involved with the work right now. I'm also elated that I've rediscovered, for myself anyway, the art of recording. I think the only thing we artists can leave behind is our recordings. Yet they are no more than a reminder of how we performed those pieces on the days we recorded them. Generally, I don't think performers leave legacies as composers do. Being remembered or forgotten by people I've never met doesn't bother me, but there's something about recording now that's made me feel a little more tranquil about my life.

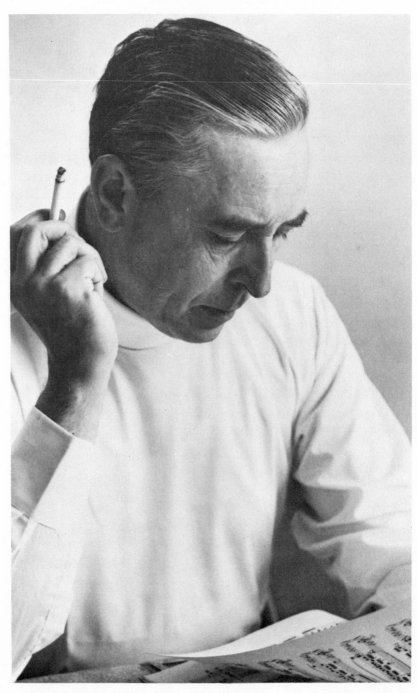

Rudolf Firkušný

RUDOLF FIRKUŠNÝ

▌▐▐▐ ▐▐ ▐▐▐ ▐▐ ▐▐▐ ▐▐ ▐▐▐ ▐▐ ▐▐▐ ▐▐ ▐▐▐ ▐▐ ▐▐▐ ▐▐ ▐

Replete with pipe and grey tweed jacket, Rudolf Firkušný could have been mistaken for a British author; but the large grand piano in the corner pointedly revealed the observer's mistake. Mr. Firkušný was most congenial, first introducing me to his wife and two children and then inviting me to sit across from him so that we could discuss his favorite topic, music. What comes through the personality of the artist is candor, positiveness, and complete devotion to his profession. Considered by many to be a musical conservative, he does not apologize for his views because he believes in the "art of music" and the "heritage of music." Unlike many other concert pianists, Mr. Firkušný did not come from a musical family. At first the piano in his home was his plaything, but gradually he came to realize that his life would be music and, once he made the selection final, there would be no turning aside whether for lack of funds or lack of teachers.

THERE was never any doubt in my mind about a choice of career. When I was three and a half or four years old, I knew I'd go into music, but I wasn't sure in what capacity. First I thought I'd be a composer; it ended with my being a pianist, probably because we had a piano at home. I'm not sure why because neither of my parents played the piano nor were they musically inclined. My mother could play a few chords on it, but that was the extent of her musical knowledge. My father died when I was three and, as far as I know, no one touched the piano until one day I began with one finger to search out a tune. I was delighted with sounds and soon the piano became my toy and a source of great delight to me. Mother didn't interfere because she thought this was my way of overcoming grief at the loss of my father; so she let me stumble around searching for more tunes. My mother couldn't help me very much, and I wasn't in school yet, so the only way I could improve myself was to find a teacher. About this time we moved from Napajedla to Brno where I tried to find a teacher, but nobody would take me because I was so small. Finally, a gentleman named Kolář took me on and began to teach me to read music. He was not a pianist, but a flutist; yet he gave piano lessons to children. I stayed with him six months just to learn a few basics so that I could continue on my own. I never took another formal piano lesson from him. I just sat at the piano and played whatever came to my mind, partly what I heard and partly what was my own inspiration or improvisation.

The word began to go around that there was a strange child in town who loved to play the piano and played all sorts of music. A bookstore owner in Brno heard the rumors and came to see me merely out of curiosity. After he heard my playing, he told my mother that he thought I was quite gifted and should be brought to someone's attention. Since neither my mother nor anyone else in the family knew much about music or the music profession, the store owner said he would arrange for composer Leoš Janáček to hear me. This came as a surprise to my mother for Janáček was known as a very difficult and severe person. In the first place, his ideas were considered too advanced for the times even in the music community, and he was already a celebrity of national stature after the great success of his opera *Jenufa* in Vienna; secondly, he had a reputation as a very hard man who among other qualities had a strong dislike for so-called "prodigies." The family thought the experience might leave me scarred. I didn't agree with them; I wanted to be a musician and, if this was the way I had to take it, I'd take it, even though I was only five.

At my insistence, they took me to Janáček who asked me to play what I could. He then tested my musical ear and told me I had perfect pitch. Next, as I faced the wall, he played chords which I identified. Now he was excited and explained to my mother that he thought I was extremely gifted and, if she would allow it, he would see to my musical education. Janáček himself would teach me musical theory and composition. As a piano teacher he recommended Miss Tučková who taught piano and harp at the "Varhanická Škola" (The Organ School) of which Janáček was director. In the beginning, I visited him twice a week. Later the visits were cut to once a week or whenever he asked to see me. I usually spent anywhere from half an hour to two hours working with him. Nothing was ever planned; each meeting was a surprise for me because everything was so spontaneous. Sometimes we sat together at the piano and played music for four hands; at other times he demonstrated works for me, like Debussy's *La Mer;* and at still other times he brought out his latest opera *Katia Kabanova,* which was almost ready for publication, put it on the music rack, and asked me to play. It certainly was an unorthodox sort of training. I really never knew for sure just what each meeting would produce. He did insist, however, that I bring him an original composition for each session. Together we went over what I had written and he showed me why he thought I had done certain sections in a particular way or why he thought they could have been done differently; but he never corrected my manuscript in the strict sense of the word. The *why* was more interesting to him than the *what.* I saved all of those early efforts because I wasn't sure yet in which direction I might go, and they could be the foundation of other compositions. I still have them, too, with Janáček's remarks written on them.

Janáček was the greatest influence on my musical life. He wasn't really the ogre that people made him out to be. He never treated me as a child, either, even though he was in his seventies and I was a subteen. Our conversations were always serious, always at an adult level. I took this to be a compliment because I saw it as a manifestation of his interest in me and in my work. I have always thought that he had a great mind musically and professionally. He insisted that I develop as a musician and not a child prodigy. I had to go to school with other children and learn the regular subjects that all youngsters learn, the more the better. Secondly, there would be no concert tours. I could play all I wanted and even in public, but tours were forbidden. He wasn't against tours as such; he simply didn't think children should be exposed to that kind of life at the risk of missing the rest of their education. Besides, he seemed adverse to the whole idea of a prodigy image. He was right.

I stayed with Janáček until I was fourteen, at which time he advised me to go to the conservatory of music to learn the old-fashioned way by studying harmony and counterpoint, etc. I did as he told me, but I still visited him and played for him whenever he asked me. I also attended his operas with him whenever one premièred. He may have been unorthodox, but he was an interesting and fascinating man.

More and more, though, I began to lean toward a career as concert pianist. From my first appearance before the public with the Czech Philharmonic Orchestra in Prague and with the conservatory orchestra in Brno, where I played Mozart's *Coronation* Concerto, I continued to appear with those orchestras every year. I also made my debut outside of Czechoslovakia in Vienna (1926), in Berlin (1927), and in Paris (1928), to outstanding critical acclaim in all the three cities, and I received a very tempting offer from a leading Viennese management (Gutmann and Knepler). On Janáček's and my teachers' advice (by then I was studying piano with Mr. and Mrs. Vilém Kurz), I did not accept it and, instead, continued my musical and general studies. As the family income was rather limited, my education was made possible by various grants and financial support from several social and charitable organizations, and later from the President of Czechoslovakia, Tomáš G. Masaryk, who also enabled me—after the completion of my studies in Czechoslovakia—to spend one year in Paris and, later, to study with Artur Schnabel.

By the time I was eighteen, I became extremely popular in my own country, Czechoslovakia, which is something of a rarity in itself. I don't think artists are usually well received in their own surroundings, probably because everyone is so familiar with them. I was the exception, and I tried to make the most of it. Young artists need

Rudolf Firkušný in a relaxed moment. *Sue A. Warek*

every opportunity they can get to play before audiences because they gain valuable experience this way and also a feeling of projection which is at the core of their art. The only possible danger I saw in the situation was that I might fall into a sense of complacency because the audiences at home would accept anything I chose to play, and I might come to think that I was much better than I actually was. It was a gratifying experience, but I began to think it was all too easy. Like the proverbial eagle, I wanted to try my wings; I would either be accepted or rejected, but I had to know. First I went to Italy and, although I was only nineteen, I was extremely well received. The critics as well as the audiences were very generous there, as they were later when I tried Paris, then London, Brussels, and other major musical centers in Europe.

Then, in 1938, came the trip to the United States for a short introductory tour. It wasn't exactly a disaster, but it certainly didn't go well, either. In the first place, I wasn't ready for it and, in the second place, I was undergoing a personal crisis that should have kept me from playing at all. I had just lost an uncle of whom I was particularly fond, and his death grieved me very much. Emotionally I was in a turmoil, and I should have let the piano alone for a while. But what was worse, I think, was my preconceived notion that American audiences were more interested in technical display, so I chose a program that was not right for me at this time. I don't regret the experience; it did me a lot of good professionally and personally. When I arrived home, political trouble was beginning to brew. In 1939, the Germans occupied Czechoslovakia and, although I was in no direct danger, I had to make a difficult decision: Should I stay in my native country with my people and bow to the will of the Nazis or should I try to continue my career elsewhere? I chose to leave and managed to get to Paris for another concert, but soon the entire world was at war. I knew I couldn't return home, so when France collapsed I fled to Portugal and then to the United States. It seemed like a wild adventure at the time. When I took stock of things in the States, I realized that I had to start again from zero, from scratch, because nobody here really knew me and because I had had the previous unsuccessful experience.

At the same time, the new start wasn't going to be especially traumatic because I had been through it all before and I had some knowledge of how to go about it. Friends took me in and, in 1941, with the help of a Russian organization presided over by Countess Tolstoy, daughter of the great Russian author, a debut recital was arranged in Town Hall. Critically speaking, the recital was a success; all seven papers in New York gave me excellent reviews, and Columbia Artists Management offered me a contract. In spite of my successful debut in New York, the beginnings in the United States were rather slow. In 1943, I was engaged by Bernardo Iriberri for an introductory tour of six concerts in South America and that turned into one of the greatest successes of my career. Instead of the originally planned six concerts, I stayed to play over eighteen and the audience and press response was truly sensational. That had repercussions also in the American press, namely, the *New York Times,* which accelerated the development of my career in the United States and brought me engagements with the leading orchestras (New York Philharmonic, Philadelphia, Boston, Chicago, among others). In spite of playing great numbers of concerts, I needed—and I need to this day—to study and learn new repertory.

Careers should always be progressing. And I like to read, especially books about musicians, like the Mozart letters which contain direct references to and ideas about his own music and that of his contemporaries. I'm still an opera buff, probably the influence of Janáček, too. I like all operas because, besides enjoying the music, I also appreciate good stage performances. Good plays interest me very much. The traveling that goes with my profession has many advantages, too. Wherever I go, whether it's America or Europe, I try to seek out interesting places or interesting people, and I try to broaden my interest in any way I can. With the great race for perfection going on, pianists are spending more and more hours practicing rather than doing other things which are as important as the hours at the keyboard. Every artist develops some kind of personality and inevitably it comes through in the performance. There's no question about the impressiveness of virtuoso display, but if that's all the pianist has to give, there's obviously something missing in the performance. The depth and breadth of the whole person are definitely necessary for interpreting any composition properly.

I try to avoid the word *technique* here because I think my definition differs from that of most musicians. Technique is usually considered in terms of speed and accuracy of playing; it is also usually associated with certain pieces of music such as Liszt's études, Chopin's études, or Rachmaninoff's concerti. But I believe you need as much technique to play a soft note in a Mozart andante as you need for some stormy passage in a Liszt rhapsody or some such piece. Technique is a combination of many factors—control, pedaling, touch, phrasing. Obviously, if you're going to play difficult pieces, you have to have the physical equipment for the performance and a knowledge of basics which is taken for granted.

I don't even like to discuss physical apparatus because it's like walking; you do it your way because it is *your* way, and because it has to be done. You develop a certain technique as part of your background, and there it is. It is you, but it is just a beginning, a start. If it's in you, you open new rings; you expand. It's a means to an end. Some young artists—Perahia is a good example—have the kind of technique I'm talking about. The digital and general surface brilliance are there, but the listener gets the feeling that it goes deeper. There's substance behind it. I've heard other young pianists, too, who seem to know what they're doing, but just how soon they'll be recognized is hard to say.

Our way of life is not an easy one. Besides the tiredness which accompanies the incessant travel, there's also the developing of an attitude which must constantly keep the performer going. I can't allow myself to look at my career or any part of it as just a job. I tell myself that each performance will be a challenge to my abilities. In the first place, I don't particularly care for plane travel. Speed isn't good for me because I can't gain my composure when I have to hurry so much. I preferred travel by train so that I had time to read, compose a few bars of music, or do anything else I wanted to allow me to wind down after a performance so that I might gradually get myself ready for the next one. I don't always look forward to the next performance with great anticipation, but I do consider it a challenge. Sometimes I'm unaware of the quality of an orchestra, or I'm unfamiliar with the conductor; sometimes also I don't know what kind of instrument I'll be playing. All these cause anxiety; so far, however, I've managed to prepare myself psychologically for any eventuality.

I guess I'll always suffer from nervousness and a bit of stage fright. In fact, I think they are increasing because, as I grow older, I feel more responsibility toward my music and my audience, so the feeling of tension increases. The tenseness, however, varies in approach and in intensity. Sometimes it starts days ahead of the concert, sometimes on the day itself, and sometimes just before going on stage; but it is always there. There have been occasions on which I've felt totally relaxed; the piano is in excellent condition, I'm rested, and it's not the kind of concert that will make or break me. I even look forward to getting started. Then all of a sudden comes the tension, and I feel more nervous than I would preceding a concert at Carnegie Hall. On other days, I feel very tired; I'm tempted to cancel the concert because it will surely come off badly. Yet somehow I get on stage to the piano and suddenly everything blossoms beautifully into a good performance. How and why this happens is as much a mystery to psychoanalysts as it is to the artists. The problem has been examined on all sides and from all angles, but no satisfactory answer has ever been offered. Usually we are told that the performer has done his homework well and has had so much experience that he is borne along by some sort of subconscious programming. In my case, once the program is under way, everything falls into place. I rest on the afternoon of a concert, then concentrate entirely on the music. I try to be totally oblivious to the presence or absence of an audience; the music becomes the center of my attention. I tell myself that each concert is a first; I try to pretend that I'm doing the work for the first time before a completely new audience, whether they be very knowledgeable or very unsophisticated, whether they be in New York City or the smallest town in Alaska. As an artist, I am responsible first to myself. Sometimes I succeed, sometimes I don't; I'm human, too. But I'll always do my best because I consider each performance a new experience, one to build on. Even if I play the same notes, the same tempi, the same dynamics, there must always be some distinctive quality to each performance that makes it different. That is my challenge.

For the same reason, I'm not particularly fond of recording because, once the record is cut, the music is there, forever the same. Any artist tries to make the best recording he can; no one wants to listen to his work later and have to apologize for it. On the other hand, no matter how well it's done, it loses its inspiration after a time because the listener knows what's there and how it's presented. At a concert, the artist can always do something, perhaps insert a nuance here or there, that makes the music alive. It is this vitality that makes me enjoy my profession. I love music, and music should live, but it can only live by a proper performance, not necessarily a technically perfect one, but one which breathes new life into it. Beethoven wrote his music to be played and heard; if you want a perfect idea of his music, you can study the score, play it in your imagination, and hear the most fantastic performance you could ever dream of, but it is still a printed score. When the pianist breathes life into it, it is then that you feel the strength and the beauty of the composition. Beethoven had to put it on paper so it would remain with us, but he never meant it only to stay there.

Today, due mainly to recordings, music has become more familiar to general audiences than in the old days, when the only listening possibilities were live concerts or amateur performances at home. There have always existed favorite artists with a great following, and nothing in this respect has changed much today. What has perhaps changed is the fact that people familiar through recordings with performances of many artists have the possibility to compare them in their minds. Every artist has something to say, even if it's different from the audience's idea of what the work *should* sound like; the audience should listen to the artist if his musical concept is a sound one.

Speaking of professional critics, they certainly are important, especially for a young artist starting a career, and also for defending a certain professional standard of performances on the concert stage. Constructive criticism can be helpful to anyone. I am my own severest critic; I am more demanding of myself than anyone else could be of me, so if I feel a criticism is unjust I shrug it off. Of course I'm human and I don't like to read unfavorable criticism; but, if I've not done well and I know I've not done well, then I'm not nearly so put out with the critic as I am with myself. Performers have to recognize that in their profession they are exposed to an entire public which has varied tastes and opinions and, whether they like the opinions or not, they are subject to them. You have to be philosophical about criticism; you shouldn't be crushed if it's unjust and, if it is just, learn from it.

When I work with my students at Juilliard, I try very hard to help each one develop his or her own individuality, especially in expression of the music. I can, of course, tell the student when something is wrong with the basics, but I don't spend any time improving fundamentals because it is supposed to be an advanced class. Besides, it's been so long since I went through the learning period that I doubt I could help them very much in that area. We work primarily with interpretation, although I know that what a student learns now he will probably change in three or four years and, I hope, do a better job of it. I can only tell my students what I think the composer had in mind, let them practice it, and see it for themselves. Nor do I pay attention to method. I don't care how they play as long as they express what they want to express. Some play better with straight fingers; others play better with curved fingers. It's the result that counts. If a sound comes out poorly, then I tell them that we will have to do something about hand stance, or wrists, or arms. Otherwise I let them alone. I don't believe in methods. Everyone's hands are different and must be worked differently. What I do with my fingers might be utterly impossible for someone else. And what someone else may do might be impossible for me. The old systems that forced everyone into the same mold are gone, too, because there are so many teachers to choose from whose methods are more free and advanced. Of course we still hear of the Russian school or the French school, which have their peculiar traditions, but their traditions followed the lines of their music more than anything else. The Russian school is more robust because the music of Rachmaninoff and Tchaikovsky is robust and consequently demands a powerful kind of expression, more on the heavy side. French music, on the other hand, is light and airy; it is very elegant and clean but a bit tempered like the works of Couperin, Rameau, Saint-Saëns, Debussy, and Ravel; it calls for a lighter touch.

When I studied under Kurz, I used a combination of the Leschetizky method, which was all fingers, and another method which emphasized body movement. I learned to use the body as an adjunct to the fingers, and I'll say this for the method: I was never tired; I could play seven or eight hours without becoming weary because I always felt somewhat loose at the keyboard. I know some pianists who tire after an hour of playing. Later, as I moved around, I experimented with new ways but rejected them because they weren't natural for me. Yet I don't think pianists ought to develop eccentricities or mannerisms just for the sake of some new technique. The artist should look comfortable at the piano. Then the audience can be attentive to the music, not the bodily movements of the artist. It's the music that counts, not the method.

Another area that I give little attention to in teaching is memory, or methods of memorizing. I am fortunate in that I was blessed with the ability to memorize quickly. It's not a photographic memory because I don't see the music; I hear it. I can't even call it a process or method because it's just there; it has been since I was ten years old. If I take on a new piece, especially in a completely different idiom, I have to study it because a different mental process is involved. If it is older music, more traditional, I sit at the piano and play it right away. I am more accustomed to the latter approach since I am more involved with traditional music than I am with contemporary. I admire contemporary music, but I don't believe I can do it justice. So most of my learning is at the piano, playing a piece until I know it. Sometimes it takes three days, sometimes a week, and sometimes a month. It all depends on how rapidly I can establish the connection between the parts and finalize the structure. But regardless of what I'm learning, I never try to force it. The knowledge of the music should come gradually and become such a part of you that you know it almost automatically. On the other hand, the music that you don't play often you forget, at least temporarily, but it usually comes back rather quickly. I don't think you ever learn a piece once and for all. It comes and it goes depending on the frequency of performances. God knows I've played the Beethoven C Minor Concerto, No. 3, many times in my life; in fact, I've recently played it on four successive occasions. Yet, if I had to play it again, I'd be practicing it as though I had not seen it in years. It won't take as much time to learn, but I'd want to start as if it were new.

I do advise practicing in a slower tempo. I think it's a good idea because, in the first place, you can overcome some bad habits which can creep into your playing. Secondly, when playing slowly, you can concentrate more on the function of the fingers and on the quality of tone than you do at a faster pace. There's a tendency generally to play faster than you should anyway because, as tension builds, the adrenalin flows more profusely and the speed of playing increases proportionately. Since this is the rule rather than the exception, it is better to back off from playing rapidly so as better to control the dynamics of the music. You know you can always come through with added power and speed. However, this applies only to practice. When I rehearse with the orchestra on the day of the concert, I always use full tone and full volume because the conductor has to balance the soloist and the orchestra, and it's important for him to know just how the soloist performs. For me, it *is* the performance, so I have to play as I would at the concert itself.

My predominant concern is always music rather than myself. I'll always remember the story my old teacher, Suk, told about himself and his entrance into heaven. The first thing he did was go over to Beethoven, drop to his knees, and kiss the composer's hands; he next went over to Wagner and made a deep bow. When he spied Mozart, he ran and hid under a table so that he wouldn't have to admit that he was a composer. If Mozart had such an effect on Suk, what is in store for lesser musicians? Perhaps we won't run and hide provided we have been true to our art. And this truth will lie not merely in the live performances we have given, but also in the recordings we made and in the legacy we leave our students. Eventually we will be judged on what we did to educate a new generation of artists to carry on the tradition that history gave us through a general attitude toward music. The art of music has persisted through the ages, and it is the job of the present artists to show the young how good that art is and to share it with them. There is so much stress today on technical efficiency that there is a danger of losing the very substance and meaning of music. We should not let this happen.

Glenn Gould. *Don Hunstein*

GLENN GOULD

Just about everything concerning Glenn Gould is, to say the least, unconventional. He is practically self-taught, he gave public, live concerts for a very brief time, yet his records and tapes are heard constantly wherever classical piano music is broadcast. His life style is unconventional. He defies tradition in his views toward his instrument, classical music, and the whole aura that surrounds the usual concept of the world of the classical pianist. Called eccentric by some, he nevertheless produces a musical sound appreciated and admired by dilettante and professional alike.

It was very natural, then, to begin the conversation with the comment that no one had heard Glenn Gould play a live concert in the United States for a number of years. His reply was typical.

NOBODY else has either because I haven't given concerts since 1964. In the first place, I toured for only eight years, which is really not very long. I didn't play in the United States, in fact, until 1955, and all I did at that time was make my debut. In the 1956–57 season, I began touring Europe as well as the United States, and that continued to '64. I had given, prior to the '56 season, a certain number of concerts in Canada every year. But I'd bet you that, before I began touring in '56, I had not in my whole life played more than maybe thirty or forty concerts; and that's really incredibly few. But I did a lot of broadcasting at that time and I found even in my early teens that, for me the most comfortable situation was the studio environment and not the concert environment.

This suggests two things, I suppose: The first is that, except in the sense of learning a lot of rather complicated repertoire very early in life, I was not a prodigy. I was not in the Menuhin mold, traveling from town to town. That didn't occur to me, and fortunately didn't occur to my parents either as something that would be advantageous. But one of the results of not traveling is that, by the time I was in my late teens, I had decided that there was something just a little bit degrading about giving concerts. The process was essentially distasteful. I did realize, however, that it was the most convenient way to make some money. And I was not immune to the prospect of making money. So, by the time I was in my early twenties, I thought I'd give concerts for a decade and by that time I'd be thirty and retire. Well, at least I came close! I retired at thirty-two! Retired, that is, from giving concerts.

From the moment I began broadcasting, *that* medium seemed like another world, as indeed it is. The moment I began to experience the studio environment, my whole reaction to what I could do with music under the proper circumstances changed totally. From then on, concerts were less than second best; they were merely something to be gotten through. They were a very poor substitute for a real artistic experience.

Now, I obviously couldn't imagine how many effects this view was going to have on my life, but I was immediately attracted to the whole electronic experience. For example, my first nationwide network broadcast, as opposed to more local ones, was in 1950, when I was seventeen. I remember, among other things, playing the Mozart Sonata, K. 281 on that particular broadcast. The studio piano actually had a rather nice sound, but a rotten action and a very thick bass; and I was very depressed about the result because I knew what I wanted from that sonata and I wasn't able to get it on that instrument. However, I took an acetate home the same day, put it on the turntable, and began to fiddle with the treble-bass control, which, of course,

was very primitive in those days. Nevertheless, I was able to minimize that thick bass by emphasizing the upper frequencies; and so
that piano became electronically altered after the fact, if you will. It
now had an altogether more appealing sound than that which I was
able to achieve under "real, live" conditions. And that experiment is
just one, rather obvious, example of many possibilities that occurred
to me during those early years as a result of my radio experience; but
it's an example that suggests not only a fondness for working in the
studio per se but also something of the ongoing nature of the electronic experience—that one's responsibility to a performance is not
finished simply because one has *given* the performance.

And the result was that I fell in love with microphones; they became friends, as opposed to the hostile, clinical inspiration-sappers
that many people think they are. One hears charges like that so often
nowadays; one *used* to hear it mainly from the older generation of
artists, such as Arthur Rubinstein perhaps. But nowadays one hears
the same thing from these twenty-year-old whippersnappers; for example, "The microphone really is depersonalizing, an instrument that
doesn't respond, gives no feedback."

During my teens, when I gave three or four concerts a year, I was
never able to enjoy or really even evaluate the audience inspiration
that one was supposed to get. When I was very young, I felt a certain
sense of power when I walked onto the stage, especially to play a
concerto. I frankly enjoyed that sort of thing when I was thirteen or
fourteen. But the enjoyment wore off rather quickly because this
mysterious, magical moment of insight that is supposed to be the net
result of the coming together of artist and audience never happened
for me. That is not to say that there were not occasional moments—
perhaps when I was giving a concert with an esteemed conductor or
playing a solo work in an especially fine hall—when some special
feeling took hold of me. I wouldn't deny that. But it didn't happen
because the audience was there; it could just as well have happened
at rehearsal or in a practice session. I can honestly say that I do not
recall ever feeling better about the quality of a performance because
of the presence of an audience. Indeed, it's precisely for that reason
that when I record, I banish everybody from the studio except the

people actually working on the recording. I used to permit spectators occasionally, when CBS would say so-and-so from *Time* magazine or some other publication wants to come and listen in. But I found that even the presence of one person would make me tend to show off and, to that extent, it actually got in the way of the performance. It meant that I was more concerned with their reaction than I was with what I was doing. Consequently, it simply did not serve the musical end. Now if you multiply that one person by two or three thousand at a large concert, you have some idea as to the extent of my reservations about public performances as an appropriate medium for music making.

After a time, about 1956 or '57, I became profoundly dissatisfied with the whole experience of giving concerts because not only did I not enjoy them per se, but my then-new experience with recording now put what I was going to do in concert in direct competition with what I could do in the studio; and I knew there was no way those two things could properly be reconciled. The recording, for me, is not a picture postcard of a concert. The attempt to record as though one is trying to capture a mystical moment in time—so-and-so at the Royal Albert Hall on a particular night with eighty-five degree temperature and ninety percent humidity—is a form of neoromanticism. Trying to capture such a mood, I think, is against the nature of the recording process because, first of all, recordings are to be a certain degree timeless. Recordings are something outside of history, outside of a particular environmental context.

The very nature of the live concert does not allow you to say, "Take two. I don't think I like what I did up to now." You know you can't do it over and yet, in my concerts, I always wanted to do exactly that. I had this incredible urge to stop, to turn around and say, "I think I'll try that again." You know, there were times when I would even have fantasies about it, but I never got up the nerve to do it. Of course, as I became more familiar with the whole process, not only of recording but of post-production, I began to do all my own editing. I don't mean in the sense of physically cutting the tape, but in terms of picking and choosing all the inserts and putting them in at every point exactly where they're going to fit.

And then, of course, in the sixties, I began producing radio documentaries in Canada that weren't necessarily related to music at all. You've got to understand that radio is alive and well in Canada; it didn't suddenly vanish with the advent of television as it did in the United States. So there is still a market for radio entertainment there. I'd had an idea of a new way to present interviews in a documentary context on the air, and so, in 1967, I put together a program almost on an experimental basis. It was called "The Idea of North," and it dealt with the reactions of five people who had for various reasons gone to the Canadian Arctic. Now these five didn't know each other; they hadn't met, nor did they have anything in common other than their experiences in the north. But I didn't simply interview them, collect alternate points of view, and present a question-and-answer show. What I wanted was a dramatic structure out of *supposed* interrelationships between them. The common theme was to be the various states of isolation. So although the materials were interview-derived, the presentation was dramatic. It was divided into a certain number of scenes with a prologue and an epilogue. With some apprehension, the network put it on the air and, despite its experimental nature, it was successful. In fact, it's been rebroadcast about twenty times in various countries and it was later turned into a film.

Meanwhile, I had begun work on a second and third program on the same theme—isolation. "The Latecomers," which had to do with life in a small out-port village in Newfoundland, was the second program in my so-called solitude trilogy, and "The Quiet in the Land" was the third. It was a rather complicated program about a Mennonite community in Manitoba. I began it, in fact, in 1971, spending many weeks interviewing the people in that community and the process of putting that one program together actually took four years.

My contract with the Canadian Broadcasting Corporation, however, specifies that I will produce a certain number of programs on musical subjects. I have, for example, done documentaries on Stokowski, Casals, Schoenberg, and Richard Strauss. But, in another respect, I guess I never really get away from music, because these programs are not the sort of linear documentaries that go from A to Z and in which possibly an announcer says, "And now, here is so-and-so.'' They're much more impressionistic. Frequently, two or even three voices are heard at the same time in what is, in effect, a contrapuntal texture. For example, at the beginning of ''The Idea of North,'' there is a trio sonata in which three people—a nurse, a geographer, and a bureaucrat—are heard speaking simultaneously. The nurse starts speaking and then the geographer comes in, and then the bureaucrat; and then the trio reverts to two voices, and then to one, and the nurse is once again alone; and that's the introduction to the program. The vocal intensity in that section is also subject to a long crescendo and diminuendo, and this particular segment occupies only about the first three or four minutes of an hour-long show. So these programs very often take on a structure that is somewhat related to music, and somewhat related to drama; I suppose they're hybrids in a way. In any event, beginning in the mid-sixties, I became a radio producer and this added another dimension to my experience of what was possible electronically. And, of course, the pleasure I took in that experience made the concert hall seem an even more inhospitable place.

Did this ''inhospitability of the concert hall'' ever cause you to feel some apprehension about playing in front of people?

Yes, but not excessively so. I used to take my pulse rate just before a concert out of scientific curiosity, and it was always very fast. So there was obviously a kind of unnatural excitement. But it wasn't the sort that paralyzed me with fear, if only because I had a kind of indifference to the whole process. I was really counting off the years and the number of events within those years that would be necessary to make it possible for me to forget the whole thing. I think if I had really been dependent upon it, or known that I had to be for a very long time, it would have depressed me so horribly that I would have been just miserable. I was, up to a point, miserable anyway, especially when I was on long tours, and particularly in Europe. But, because I viewed concerts as a means to an end, I knew I could eventually get on to the business of making music in a proper and sensible way, and that knowledge kept me going.

*Let's go back for a minute to your statement on early retirement.
How many people are able to say that they retire at thirty-two? Most
of us haven't started at thirty-two!*

I guess it all has to do with goals and priorities. In the years after
1964, I enormously accelerated my recording activities, which, until
that time, had been, as most concert artists' activities are, subservient
to what I was doing in concerts. In fact, the recordings very often
turned out to involve works that I'd try out first on audiences in the
concert hall and then record. And the recordings usually showed the
defects of that practice because, as far as I'm concerned, the most
that can be said about the concert experience is that you pick up a lot
of bad interpretative habits.

In the summer of '57, for example, I recorded the Bach Fifth Partita, the first of the partitas that I put on tape for CBS. The date is
significant only because I had just returned from my first European
tour—which consisted of concerts in Austria, Germany, and the Soviet Union—and during that tour, and during the months leading up
to it, the Fifth Partita, which is a great favorite of mine, was an integral part of almost every program. Even if it was not on the program,
its "Sarabande" or some other movement was used as an encore, so
that I had played this work, or portions of it, literally dozens of times
within a very few months. And then I went to record it.

Now, three years before it became contaminated with this concert
hall experience, I had also recorded it, not for a commercial label,
but for the overseas service of the CBC. That earlier recording is not
technically better than the one done in 1957, but it is a much more integrated concept of the music than the later version. And the reason
for that is very simple: During those concert experiences I had to project that particular piece to a very large audience in most cases and, as
a consequence, I had added hairpins—crescendi and diminuendi, and
similar un-Bachian affectations—where they didn't need to be; I had
exaggerated cadences in order to emphasize the separation of sen-
tences or paragraphs, and so on. In other words, I was making an unnecessarily rhetorical statement about the music, simply as a consequence of having attempted to project it in very spacious acoustic
environments.

In a studio, where the pick-up is close to the piano, you can achieve a very similar effect to that which the listener enjoys at home. The relationship of the piano to a microphone which is, let's say, eight feet away is very similar to the relationship between the listener at home and his speakers. There's a one-to-one aspect in both situations. But no such relationship exists when one is sitting on a stage, like the Tchaikovsky Hall in Moscow, and projecting a Bach partita to the first row of seats and to the top balcony simultaneously.

So the result was that the record made in the summer of '57 is a very glib, facile effort, because a series of little party tricks which just don't need to be there had been added to the piece. Now the interesting thing is that, at the same time, I also recorded the Sixth Partita, which I had played very rarely in public. I did play it once in the Soviet Union and, I think, maybe once or twice in Canada and the States prior to that tour, but no more. Then I recorded it, and that's a good recording. No party tricks.

As long as we're on the subject of recordings, which would you say are your finest recording accomplishments? Is there any one or two or three, or any group of things that you've done that stand out as especially good to you?

My favorite record from my own catalogue, I think, is a recording of music by Byrd and Gibbons which, first of all, *as* music, is very close to my heart. I have always been very fond of music for the virginals—indeed, of all the music of the English Tudor composers—and, fortunately, I have a piano which can be made to sound rather harpsichordistic, if not clavichordistic.

It's strange you should choose that recording. Ordinarily when one thinks of Glenn Gould, one thinks of Schoenberg and Bach. Would you say you're a specialist in those two areas, or would you not want to be labeled in any such way?

I don't mind being labeled as a specialist that way, but I think it's necessary occasionally to remind people that I have also recorded all

the Mozart sonatas, most of the Beethoven sonatas, and of course all
the Beethoven concertos, as well as a lot of things by Hindemith, and
pieces by Prokofieff, and Grieg, and Bizet, and Scriabin, and so on.
As a matter of fact, not too long ago I recorded an album of Sibelius.
He wrote quite a lot of pieces for the piano, most of which are
absolute junk. Yet there are, in their midst, works of real quality, and
I think that the three Sonatinas, which I recorded, are in that cate-
gory. They're very strange pieces because they are almost entirely
diatonic and formally almost neoclassical, which strikes one as very
odd in a post-romantic milieu (they were written between the Fourth
and Fifth Symphonies), but I think they stand up awfully well.

But actually that recording stands apart by virtue of the particular
sonic effects used in it. We recorded it on eight tracks, so that we had
four totally different two-track perspectives available—perspectives
which were then mixed like the stops of an organ. The actual production method is something that I had wanted to try for a long time,
given the right repertoire. I had experimented with it in a film for
French television some years ago when I did some Scriabin preludes
that way. It's like photographing the music sonically, as though you
treated the microphone like a camera. You "shoot" the score from
different angles, so to speak. For example, for the closest of the
perspectives, we placed microphones right inside the piano—virtually
lying on the strings—not unlike a jazz pick-up. The next perspective
was my standard one which, for many tastes, is a bit too close for
comfort. The third perspective was a sort of discreet Deutsche Gra-
maphon-style European sound, and the fourth and last was back-of-
the-hall ambiance. Now, we recorded all of these perspectives simultaneously, of course, and then selected from them, after the fact,
creating a kind of acoustic choreography in the process.

You see, I think one of the unfortunate legacies of the concert hall
which has found its way into the recording process is that we've
come to expect that a piano, for example, will be placed more or less
between the left and right speakers, and will remain there from first
note to last. In this recording of Sibelius, you very often sense that a
particular statement, a particular theme, is suddenly much farther
away from you without at the same time necessarily getting softer.

It's precisely as if you employed a zoom shot with a camera. Mind you, I think that one should not use a technique of this kind indiscriminately; it suits certain late-romantic repertoire very well indeed, and it might be equally appropriate for a Gabrieli canzona, but I certainly don't think that it would enhance a Haydn sonata.

What is it about Schoenberg's music that attracts you?

I think I was first attracted to it because some of my teachers hated it; advocacy can be a useful weapon in a teenage rebellion. Actually I've always been attracted to music that is in one way or another contrapuntal, whereas I'm essentially bored by homophonic music. Indeed, I've often said that I have something like a century-long blind spot with regard to music. It's roughly demarcated by *The Art of the Fugue* on one side and *Tristan* on the other, and almost everything in between is, at best, the subject of admiration rather than love. I'd have to exclude Beethoven from that generalization and certain works of Haydn and Mendelssohn, but there's a great deal of music written during that time that I don't play at all—Schubert, Chopin, Schumann, for example. When my recording of the complete Mozart sonatas was released recently, I devoted about seven thousand words to explaining why I really don't like Mozart's music very much. And one of the main reasons, certainly, is that it's not especially contrapuntal and worked out, so to speak. When I have to deal with such music, I confess that I tend to emphasize tenor parts to alto parts—anything to give it the semblance of a contrapuntal presence, to give it the illusion of a polyphonic lay-out.

And my tastes in contemporary music, similarly, are really very limited. I cannot bear Stravinsky, for example; I've never been able to tolerate his music. And his music certainly is vertically oriented to a very high degree, and only minimally interesting from the horizontal perspective. By comparison, the integration between line and harmonic balance is very apparent in the best of Schoenberg's works; in fact, one could say that the pursuit of that kind of integration is one of Schoenberg's trademarks, and I'm not just speaking of the twelve-tone works. But as far as what attracts me is concerned, I guess I'd

Glenn Gould at a recording session

have to say that I'm attracted to different aspects of his art at different periods of his life. In the early years, the tonal years, I suppose it's the element of what you might call musical "brinksmanship"—a chromaticism that tests the limits of tonality but which is not used gratuitously and which, in fact, is the logical result of the most intense use of counterpoint in all of post-romantic music. And I think those pieces are incredibly misunderstood, even today; I think *Pelléas and Mélisande* is at least as good as any of Strauss's tone-poems—and that's saying a great deal because I love Strauss—and the E Major Chamber Symphony is simply in a class by itself.

I'm less interested, I must say, in the works written around the First World War, where he's no longer writing tonally but is not yet using the twelve-tone system either. Certainly, there are one or two masterpieces from that period—*Erwartung* particularly—but I must admit that *Pierrot Lunaire* drives me up the wall and always has. Besides, I don't think Schoenberg was cut out for a career as a miniaturist. I think things like the Six Little Piano Pieces, Opus 19, for all the influence they had on other composers—Webern and so on—are, in Schoenberg's case, anyway, the reflection of a great insecurity as to where he was going musically at that time. I should add, by the way, that I don't think any of his best works are for the piano, including the Concerto, and that's probably because Schoenberg tended to use the piano as a quick and dirty medium for the trying out of new techniques. But I do think that the Piano Suite, Opus 25 is a marvelous piece, all the same. It's the first work with a tone-row used throughout. Portions of the Serenade, Opus 24 and the Five Piano Pieces, Opus 23 have rows, but the Suite uses a row from first note to last—so once again, the piano is used for a major experiment.

But, experiments aside, I find the mood of those early twelve-tone pieces remarkable. They have a charm and freshness of approach which is quite extraordinary. Schoenberg was not exactly renowned for a sense of humor but suddenly, and rather briefly, in the twenties, he seems to have discovered a latent witty streak that's really very attractive. I'm not a die-hard believer in the twelve-tone system, however; I tend to admire Schoenberg in spite of it rather than because of it. But it did, undeniably, satisfy the Germanic urge toward what one might call visual as well as aural coherence in music and, perhaps for that reason, it made Schoenberg, if only temporarily, a very happy man.

The later works, on the other hand, the ones written in America—the piano and violin concertos, and things like that—I find rather obvious and mechanical, not to mention humorless. I find that the architecture is a little too predictable and I really don't think that one can successfully adapt the twelve-tone system to sonata allegro form, for example. That isn't what it's meant to do. But that, in the later years anyway, is what Schoenberg did in effect. The problem, to put it in the lingo of tape-editing, is that one can see the splices going through.

From what you have just said, what do you think music will be like in the next fifty or hundred years, that is, what do you think composers are going to compose or create?

Well, predictions in music are as difficult as predictions in any other area, and I don't know if I have any worth making. It would seem to me, however, that one really can't be sure that serious music, with quotation marks around serious, is going to exist indefinitely in its present form. It's pretty obvious, and I'm not saying anything at all original, that the particular kind of sonic organization that the Germanic traditions emphasized, and which the eighteenth and nineteenth centuries, in particular, represented, is more or less at an end.

I suspect that there will be temporary moves in one direction or another; right now, for example, there is a kind of reconciliatory impulse abroad in which certain kinds of nostalgic tonal elements are coming back in a quite interesting context. There may very well be some kind of merger between musical sound and spoken sound. I don't mean a merger in any operatic sense. I'm thinking of something that relates to my own special interest—documentaries that are part musical compositions, part drama, for example. They represent a synthesis of various disciplines in which certain abstract elements or pure structure are wedded to certain very concrete elements of objective fact. But, in any event, I don't think of myself as a prophet, and

I really can't answer your question with any accuracy, except to say that I sometimes have really very grave doubts about the continued happy existence of music as a separate state in the context of the so-called arts.

What about the format, the representation, for example, of the recital? There are rumors that the recital format is out, or at least is on the way out.

Well, I don't go to concerts—I rarely did, even when I was giving them, and as a matter of fact the last concert I attended was in 1967—so I can't honestly tell you that such a format has no validity in today's scheme of things. But it doesn't for me, certainly; as far as I'm concerned, music is something that ought to be listened to in private. I do not believe that it should be treated as group therapy or any other kind of communal experience. I think that music ought to lead the listener—and, indeed, the performer—to a state of contemplation, and I don't think it's really possible to attain *that* condition with 2,999 other souls sitting all around. So my strongest objections to the concert are primarily moral rather than musical. But as far as the format of the recital is concerned, I personally don't particularly relish a sequence of the same instrumental sounds all evening, especially if they're piano sounds. There are, as you well know, many piano freaks. I just don't happen to be one of them. I don't much care for piano music.

You don't care much for music from the instrument you play? That's hard to believe.

Well, I'm really not hooked on the instrument per se—on any instrument, per se. I'm kind of instrumentally indifferent, I guess. Of course, if I hear a very scintillating performance I get great pleasure from it; I certainly don't mean to say that I don't get pleasure from listening to performances that involve the piano, but I don't get pleasure from performances *because* they involve the piano. And I think that that really has always been true. I've never been a piano buff in that sense.

Whose recordings do you listen to? Whom do you admire who's recording today?

Oh, my goodness! That's one of those awful questions. If I say A and B, I'm probably overlooking C and D, so please don't regard this as anything like the definitive short list. But if I think only of pianists to whom I've been listening with some regularity and great pleasure recently, I'd have to mention the Mozart concerto recordings of Alfred Brendel. I happen not to like the Mozart concertos. I don't believe any of them really work as structures; yet, I find that Brendel's recordings come as close to making them work as any that I've heard.

I find that in the late-romantic works—which again is not an area that I'm particularly interested in—I like Alexis Weissenberg's playing very much indeed. He made an absolutely marvelous recording of a piece that I would normally never sit down and listen to—the Rachmaninoff Second Concerto; but in the case of his recording, which is conducted by von Karajan, I've listened to it at least three or four times and I find that it's really a most penetrating look at Rachmaninoff, more penetrating, perhaps, than Rachmaninoff deserves. Weissenberg takes an essentially classical look at something that is almost always played too romantically and, as a result, one is not aware that this is a great virtuoso recreating yet another performance of a warhorse; one is not aware of any exaggerated sense of competitive challenge between piano and orchestra, between soloist and conductor. One is aware, rather, of a complete integration of the solo part within the structure and, however deficient that structure may be, I nevertheless find that an extraordinary interpretative achievement.

What about Bach?

Well, you know, the only pianist who had any kind of influence on me when I was growing up—vis-à-vis the Bach repertoire—was Rosalyn Tureck. I have a great admiration for her principally because, back in the forties when I was a student, one was told one must look for guidance regarding Bach interpretation to figures like Edwin Fischer, Landowska, Casals, and so on. And these were late-romantic figures who certainly played in a very mesmeric way—no question about it. But what they did, for the most part, didn't seem to me to have a great deal to do with Bach. And then I heard Tureck. By the time I heard her recordings, I was, I think, about sixteen. As far as I know, those were recordings made in the late forties, and I don't believe I heard her play at all before I was in my mid-teens. By that time, my own style was quite formed—spare, unpedaled; and then I heard somebody else who was doing something essentially similar and I said, "Yeah! To hell with all these pedagogues who tell you that's not the way to do it. You *can* do it that way. It's marvelous." And so my exposure to her recordings was not perhaps so much a question of influence as of reinforcement; it was nice to know that somebody else was working in essentially the same direction. I must say that I found her tempi then, as I do now, unnecessarily slow most of the time; but that didn't really matter because the relationship between the parts, both in terms of architectural parts and linear parts, was so well thought out that tempo became a relative, essentially unimportant matter, subservient to something else.

Did you ever get to try your theories on the relativity of tempi?

Yes, on several occasions. One such had to do with a recording I made, with Stokowski, of the *Emperor* Concerto. But the incident itself cannot be completely understood without some background. There are certain conventions in playing the piano that infuriate me, and the logic of which I do not understand. Basically, for example, I don't like concertos, and the reason I don't like them is that I don't believe in a musical structure that derives its impetus from the spirit of competition. As a consequence, I've recorded relatively few concertos, considering the size of my discography. Anyway, in the case of the *Emperor* recording, my goal was to demythologize, so to speak, the virtuoso aspect of the concerto, to try and take away the soloist/orchestra rivalry and integrate what the soloist is doing with what the orchestra is doing. Usually, you know, it's a matter of "you play your theme and then I'll play my theme, and I'll do it slower, faster, subtler, whatever, than you." My idea was to create a sense of tempo continuity within all of the movements—the outer movements, in particular—which would get rid of those ridiculous tugs and pulls between conductor and soloist and treat the work like a symphony with piano obligato.

Now, as far as the basic tempi themselves were concerned, such matters, as I said with regard to Tureck a moment ago, are relatively unimportant. It does not occur to me to insist that there is *a* tempo for a Beethoven concerto, or any concerto, but rather that there is perhaps a tempo that will work in relation to a particular concept. But you first have got to get the concept, and the concept doesn't usually come through the tempo, as far as I'm concerned; the tempo serves the concept. Anyway, when I recorded the *Emperor,* I got together with Stokowski five days before the recording and, when he asked what my tempo was, I replied that I didn't have a tempo, that I was prepared to put two tempi at his disposal. One was very slow and one was very fast, and I wanted to try out both on him. In fact, I *had* a strong preference, but I was willing to do whatever he wanted to do. And so I played him the opening tutti of the first movement, very slowly at first and then much faster. And then I did the same sort of thing with the last movement; and he much preferred the slow version, as, indeed, did I. What we wanted to create was a sense of integrated thematic structure that would minimize or, as I said before, demythologize the virtuoso role. Naturally, there are obvious exceptions—I didn't play the cadenza exactly in tempo—but, by creating harmonious relationships instead of rivalries, I think we were able to rid the concerto of a lot of the exhibitionistic impulses that I find inappropriate in music. To sum it all up, tempi per se don't much matter to me as long as there is an organic relationship that is established between motivic units.

But do you think that if Beethoven came back to life he'd go along with these notions of motif and tempo?

I don't really know, nor do I very much care, but I'll speculate for you. I think that we don't need to go as far back as Beethoven's time to know that certain notions about tempi seem to be abroad in various lands at various times and seem to reflect relatively local or temporary concerns.

For example, I came across a very interesting sentence in Erich Leinsdorf's autobiography which amazed me when I first read it. I can't quote it exactly, but he was talking about the thirties, particularly in America, and he said something to the effect that, in those days, the tempi were very much faster in general than they are today. And, as I began to think about it, I listened, with that sentence in mind, to whichever recordings I encountered from that era; and it's true! On the other hand, there seems to be an ability nowadays, on the part of most audiences, to tolerate great, long expanses of music—an ability that seems not to have existed thirty or forty years ago. As recently as the forties and early fifties, it was just about unheard of, outside of Austria and Germany and possibly Holland, for audiences to willingly sit still for a Bruckner or Mahler symphony, as you know. But nowadays, nobody thinks twice about it. Moreover, very often the music is played at absolutely funereal tempi. One could further speculate, somewhat interestingly, I think, about the disposition of live audiences and record listeners to sit still for an hour or more to hear the "psychedelic" music of the sixties. And what do they hear? Not just one mood, but one chord or one progression, perhaps—I'm thinking of things like Stockhausen's *Stimmung* or Riley's *In C,* which is boring as hell to me. But, nevertheless, it obviously is possible for listeners today to find some kind of pleasure in the continuity of one mood for a long span of time.

Now, in Beethoven's time, we know that audiences had an incredible ability to endure unbelievably long concerts that would not be tolerated by most listeners today. Whether they had a similar ability to endure continuities of tempi, of course, is another question; from the nature of the music, one would be inclined to doubt it. It would seem more likely, again from the nature of the music, that Bach's audiences, on the other hand, probably did have that ability.

With all of our discussion of Glenn Gould, the musician, we've heard little about Glenn Gould, the person. What are you like outside the recording studio? What is your life style?

First of all, I can't divorce the studio from my personal life. The recording studio and the kind of womblike security that it gives is very much integrated with my life style. I guess it's all part of my fantasy to develop to the fullest extent a kind of Howard Hughesian secrecy. I'm a very private person, I think. I'm alone, or quasi-alone, a lot because the recording studio, with its small crew, provides me with the atmosphere that I need to work productively—to make music or, indeed, to work on a radio or television program. I stay up all night mostly. I very rarely go to bed until five or six o'clock in the morning, and it's not unusual for me to hear the headlines on the "Today Show" before turning in. I tend to get up around three in the afternoon.

This schedule gradually evolved over a period of many years. During my concert-giving days, I either went to bed early, if I had a concert the next day, or late if I had one the night before. So, in the early years, my schedule was very erratic; but thereafter I gradually became a night person. I have a rather delightful studio in Toronto where I do a lot of my editing, late, late at night, sometimes working all night until the crack of dawn.

What do you do when you aren't recording?

The first thing you've got to realize is that not more than about fifty percent of the things I do, in terms of my working life, are related to music as such. Let's take the example of the radio programs I mentioned. When you do something like that, the actual amount of studio time involved is enormous. The reason, in fact, that I have my own studio here is precisely because the CBC got fed up indulging me when I would ask for five or six hundred hours of studio time to do a program. So we finally came to an agreement where they said, "Look, you go ahead, buy your own equipment, set up a studio and do the programs, but we don't want to see you until everything's done because we can't keep on giving you this kind of time." They're such complicated programs that they really necessitate those seemingly extravagant amounts of studio time. In addition, because of all the writing I do, and so on, I really do not use more than fifty percent of my time for music—rather less than that, in fact, because I do almost no practicing at all really.

A few years ago, I was astonished to read the Barbra Streisand article which you wrote for High Fidelity.

I've written articles on all kinds of topics from politics to popular singers. I did a piece years ago, which I'm really very proud of, called "The Search for Petula Clark." Of course, it was not really a search for Petula Clark at all. I used her as a jumping off point in order to examine the whole so-called flower-child generation of the mid-sixties.

And in the case of Barbra Streisand, the article was really just a declaration of my inordinate fondness for her music making, and it was tied into a review of the *Classical Barbra* album. I think I was the only person who reviewed it favorably. I adore everything she does. Well, almost everything—there are a few albums where she attempted a sort of pseudo-rock chic which I found offensive. But then I find all rock music offensive; always have. It's so simpleminded; I can't understand things that are that uncomplicated.

But Streisand is extraordinary. I don't know of any other singer, with the exception of Elizabeth Schwarzkopf, who has impressed me as much. I was guest-hosting a program for the CBC a couple of years ago—a sort of two-hour disc jockey show—and I spent an hour, one afternoon, talking about Streisand and playing various cuts from her albums because I wanted to make the point that there are, all other aspects notwithstanding, certain similarities between Streisand and Schwarzkopf. I think they're both, first of all, italicizers; they both tend to draw attention to rather unexpected details—minute enharmonic inflections, for example—and they both do this in what I'm quite sure is a carefully, indeed, meticulously preplanned fashion, but manage to make it sound as though the notion occurred to them on the spur of the moment. I really can't think of any experience to equal Schwarzkopf's italicizations in the last scene of Strauss's Capriccio except perhaps Streisand's singing of something like Dave Grusin's "A Child is Born." There are two descending scales, in different modes, in that song and to hear Streisand inflect them—well, it's just unbelievable, it's spell-binding. It's very hard to find words to say why something moves one as much as that moves me.

By the way, I mentioned being a guest disc jockey, and I must say that's just about the most fun there is. I've always wanted to read the CBC news, for example. I'll never be allowed to because newscasters have a very tight union, but I would love to do it. I can't think of any more fun than being Walter Cronkite for a day.

What about your views in areas other than music? Your views, for example, on a life hereafter?

I can only say that I was brought up as a Presbyterian; I stopped being a church-goer at the age of about eighteen, but I have had all my life a tremendously strong sense that, indeed, there is a hereafter, and the transformation of the spirit is a phenomenon with which one must reckon, and in the light of which, indeed, one must attempt to live one's life. As a consequence, I find all here-and-now philosophies repellent. On the other hand, I don't have any objective images to build around my notion of a hereafter, and I recognize that it's a great temptation to formulate a comforting theory of eternal life, so as to reconcile one's self to the inevitability of death. But I'd like to think that's not what I'm doing; I'd like to think that I'm not employing it as a deliberate self-reassuring process. For me, it intuitively seems right; I've never had to work at convincing myself about the likelihood of a life hereafter. It is simply something that appears to me infinitely more plausible than its opposite, which would be oblivion.

Surrounding any prominent person such as yourself, there is always a good deal of myth, or legend, and a good deal of truth. The two stories that readily pop into my mind are the "glove myth" and the "broken chair myth." Is either true?

Well, sometimes the truth is almost legend. But let's take the "glove myth" first. I usually wear gloves all year round when I go out-doors—same thing with scarves. But I certainly do not sit around in-doors with them on unless it's an unusually cold room. All of these bits of tantalizing copy really date from my earliest days with CBS, when we would occasionally allow someone from the press to attend a recording session—something that I have not permitted for many years; and the recording booth was usually arctically air-conditioned while the studio itself was rather warm. So I'd simply put on a scarf and gloves when listening to playbacks. And this perfectly simple precautionary measure was blown up into a very elaborate series of rituals. In no time at all, it became part of what everybody had to write about when describing what I did, and it gradually evolved into the most ridiculous series of stories.

To set the rest of the record absolutely straight, I admit to having played one concert wearing not only a scarf but an overcoat as well as a pair of gloves that were cut so that my fingers could protrude. It happened during a series of concerts with the Israel Philharmonic in 1958. We arrived in Jerusalem a few hours before the concert, only to discover that there was no heat whatsoever. It wasn't that the heat wasn't on. There simply was no heating system in this particular hall. It was about forty-five degrees outside and perhaps fifty inside. I don't know how they stood it, but I couldn't. And I said, "Look, I really can't play here. You're going to have to put on a symphony in place of the concerto, because, otherwise, I'll catch one hell of a cold, and what good will I be on the tour?" Well, as it happened, they didn't have any substitute orchestral parts available and, con-sequently, there was a compromise about my attire. The master of ceremonies came out and made a speech explaining what was going to happen. I then walked out amid great laughter in my overcoat with my scarf around my neck. I don't think I had my hat on, but I did have, indeed, these gloves that left the fingers free. Then I played the Beethoven Second Concerto and that was that. But, thereafter, all sorts of news copy indicated that I played virtually *every* concert wearing something of the sort and, of course, once a story of that sort begins to circulate, there's very little that one can do about it. It tends to take on a life of its own.

Then what about this chair that you use? At Orchestra Hall in Chicago you had this chair, too.

I've always had that chair. I use it because I cannot bear to sit on any surface that is not conducive to my way of playing the piano. First of all, I will not sit on any surface that has any kind of "give" to it while I play and that eliminates all conventional piano benches. That chair, by the way, has now totally lost what was left of its seat; in my touring days it was stomped on by somebody during shipment in an airplane. So I now use only the frame of the chair, and it's amazing that it's not uncomfortable; but it really isn't. I have used the same chair for every concert, and every recording, and every practice session since 1953. As you know, I sit very low at the keyboard and, although this chair is only fourteen inches off the floor that's still a bit too high for comfort, and so I put a block under each of the casters of the piano to raise the instrument about an inch and a quarter—which, effectively, puts me thirteen inches from the floor. I don't understand, frankly, how anybody can play the piano at the conventional heights which are afforded by ordinary benches, and I certainly don't understand the function that such heights are alleged to serve. To me, control increases in direct relationship to one's proximity to the keyboard. When you see someone come out on stage and sit down on one of those adjustable bench things, and then go up and down looking for the perfect resting spot, it's obvious that they couldn't possibly be at the same hair's breadth measurement for their seating at any two consecutive concerts. With my system, I'm always at the same height; I haven't changed by an eighth of an inch in well over twenty years.

Did you learn any of this from a teacher? Or your parents, perhaps?

Not really, no. My mother was my first teacher. She taught me from the time I was three until I was ten. She herself played the piano and also sang a bit; but her musical activities were pretty much directed to conducting church choirs and things like that. Subsequently, the only piano teacher I had was Alberto Guerrero. I studied with him until I was nineteen, and thereafter only with myself. Guerrero was a very interesting man in many respects and had some interesting thoughts about playing the piano. The most interesting thing he did, I think, was to let a student, if he believed in him, disagree and go his own way. He would occasionally get very upset with the ideas the student might put forward, but he allowed such disagreements to fall where they might. And so, by the time I was in my mid-teens, most of my musical attitudes and all of my pianistic ones with but one exception—that of the height question, of my actual relationship to the keyboard—were already quite formed.

My studies with Guerrero, in my later teens, were essentially exercises in argument—they were attempts to crystallize my point of view versus his on some particular issue, whatever it was, and therefore a useful exercise. I dare say, with some students, that kind of approach might not work; you could very easily be crushed by the kind of argumentative experience that a much older person can use. But if you're cocky, as I was, then it really doesn't do anything other than make you determined to prove your point of view. And I think that for me, anyway, it worked very well.

The term eccentric has been applied to you many times. How do you react to it?

I don't think that my life style is like most other people's and I'm rather glad for that; I think it's in some way integrated with the kind of work that I want to do. As I said previously, the two things, life style and work, have become one. Now if that's eccentricity, then I'm eccentric. If eccentricity consists of wearing a scarf in an air-conditioned environment while recording, or playing with an overcoat on during my stay in Jerusalem, I'm guilty; but those things are organic to what I have to do.

The three hours had passed quickly. There was much more to be learned from and about this man who, in his own words, "preferred

*to exist as far as possible from the outside world and have contact
with it electronically''; but some areas would have to be left for
another time. Achieving fame as a classical pianist primarily through
the medium of records is no mean attainment, but to Glenn Gould,
eccentric or not, it is his way.*

Vladimir Horowitz. *Bill Ray*

VLADIMIR HOROWITZ

I III II III II III II III II III II III II III II I

During his ten-day visit to Chicago, Vladimir Horowitz and his wife Wanda (daughter of famed conductor Arturo Toscanini) stayed in the sumptuous suite normally occupied by Sir Georg Solti at the Drake Hotel. It was a late Friday afternoon in October, several days after the maestro had played the first of two unforgettable recitals at Orchestra Hall.

Horowitz entered the living room, expressing apologies for the slight delay. Relaxed and in jovial spirits, he extended greetings accompanied by a generous handshake. I couldn't help noticing his huge maroon bow tie, which was only overshadowed by his smile of equal proportions. Horowitz is a rather small, almost wiry man. Yet, to his peers and public alike, he is truly a giant at the keyboard, and perhaps the most influential pianist of this century. After seating himself on the long sofa, he began to relate his views on what he loves best, namely, music. His first remarks were directed toward what he believes to be the substance of pianism.

The music is behind the notes, not under them. As Arthur Nikisch once said, "You can play these notes as you would a typewriter; but where is the music? The music is behind the notes. The sense of the music is that when you open the score, the spirit of the music comes out the other side of the ledger, not from this side." You have to open the music, so to speak, and see what's behind the notes because the notes are the same whether it is the music of Bach or someone else. But behind the notes something different is told and that's what the interpreter must find out. He may sit down and play one passage one way and then perhaps exaggerate the next, but, in any event, he must do something with the music. The worst thing is not to do anything. It may even be something you don't like, but do it! The printed score is important, but the interpretation of it has been the object of my life study.

I don't mean to disparage the role of intellect, however. It is important for the musician to learn as much about the composer as possible and to study the music he has written. Then even a short piece by Brahms or Chopin can be played with much more understanding. Equally important is that the musician must immerse himself in the cultural period that produced the work he studies and plays. He should be acquainted with the painting, poetry, and music of the times—all music, not just piano repertoire. I remember a young man who came to play for me. He had prepared the Rachmaninoff-Paganini Variations and asked if I would listen to it. I persuaded Mrs. Horowitz to go into the garden and listen to him and then give me her opinion of his performance of the work. After he finished playing, I asked him whether he had ever read a book on Rachmaninoff's life, and he replied in the negative. The boy didn't known a damn thing about Rachmaninoff or Paganini for that matter. He had a number of degrees from distinguished universities, but the young man had never read about the character of the composer; nor was he at all acquainted with the literature of the period. Like some pianists today, he had a tendency to play the piano percussively; and if the piano is played only in this manner, it is a bore. If I attend a concert and someone plays like that, I have two choices: to go home or to sleep!

So the most important thing is to make a percussive instrument a. singing instrument. Teachers should stress this aspect in their instruction, but it seems that very few of them actually do. The few who try aren't always understood by the students. One way in which I obtain a singing quality is by using the damper pedal frequently; but you don't hear it. When, in changing from one chord to the next, the damper pedal remains depressed long enough so that there is an overlapping of the two harmonies for a moment, a singing quality, the result of the legato pedaling, is produced. No other instrument in the orchestra is capable of doing that.

Then there is the question of technique. So frequently am I asked about this so-called phenomenal technique which I have; but I have no phenomenal technique. There is that technique, the ability to play scales rapidly up and down the keyboard, which is necessary, but which becomes very boring after two or three minutes of listening. You see that piano over in the corner? That instrument is capable of sounds which are loud and soft; but in between there are many, many degrees of sounds which may be played. To be able to produce many varieties of sound, now that is what I call technique, and that is what I try to do. I don't adhere to any methods because I simply don't believe in them. I think each pianist must ultimately carve his own way, technically and stylistically.

What other advice that you adhere to in your own playing would you offer to aspiring pianists?

One suggestion I would offer is never to imitate. There is an old Chinese proverb which says, "Do not seek to follow in the master's footsteps; seek what he sought." Imitation is a caricature. Any imitation. Find out for yourself. When I was fifteen or sixteen and sought to learn much of the Wagner repertoire, I went to sleep with *Götterdämmerung* under my pillow. I was more interested in *Götterdämmerung* than in playing Bach Preludes and Fugues at that time. My mother was going out of her mind. She would go to my teacher and complain to him that I was playing *Götterdämmerung* instead of my piano pieces. My teacher would reply, "Let him do what he wants."

Another bit of advice would be that the pianist should never be afraid to take risks. When I play for audiences, I take risks. Sometimes they're correct, sometimes they are not. But I am not afraid to

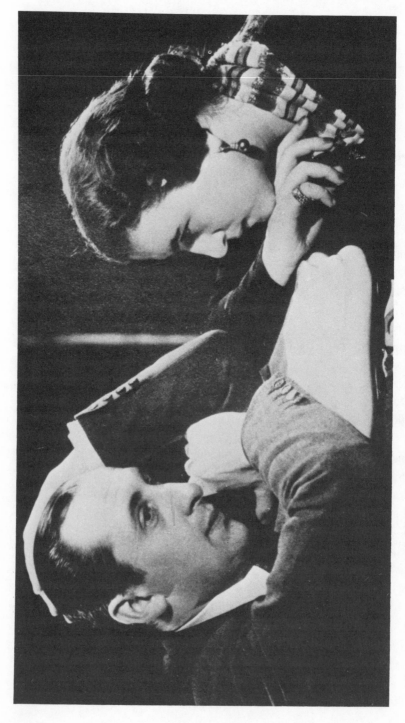

Vladimir Horowitz and his wife Wanda, photographed by Cecil Beaton in 1934

take risks if I need to in order to bring through the correct spirit of the work.

Perhaps, too, I can say that a work should never be played the same way. I never do. I may play the same program from one recital to the next, but I will play it differently, and because it is always different, it is always new.

What change has there been since your sabbatical from performing? It has been said that your playing has mellowed since earlier days.

Like good wine, I've mellowed a bit. Perhaps in these later years there has also been a change in some of my attitudes. Before, I was always aware there was a public in the hall, and I played to please the public. You know, pleasing the public is not always an easy task. In the thirties, I played so many concerts, and often my manager would tell me that I played too serious a program. For example, he asked me to take out the Chopin G Minor Ballade because it was too difficult for the public at that time. Then at times he told me I was playing "too dry." How did they expect me to play? Wet? Consequently, I tried playing for the public, and I selected music that I thought would be pleasing to them. Times are different now. Today I play the music I want and I just try to do my best.

Another change has been that I now do exactly what I want to do, and when I choose to do it. If I feel like it, I can play three concerts a year or I can play twenty. Before I was always entangled with management, fulfilling obligations, discussing business affairs, and things like that. Now that's all over with, and that's what I'm very happy about. If I want to play in New York, I do; If I want to play five times, I play five times. I make the decision. I've also simplified business arrangements by making all the concerts I play single admission. They're not part of a series. I also continue to insist on afternoon concerts because that's when I'm freshest and I believe it is also the best time for the audience.

Life is very busy now. I find that in today's cities the public is very tired after working the whole day. When concerts start at eight o'clock, the wife pushes the husband to go to the concert where some will promptly fall asleep! I think the best time to schedule such a concert is between four and six o'clock in the afternoon. Not only is my mind the best then, but audiences are more content to attend concerts at that time of day, and they are more alert and relaxed, too.

I also find a certain magic in the afternoon, inexplainable, but nevertheless there. Naturally, this is one of the reasons why I stopped playing with orchestras, since they usually play in the evening. Also, playing with orchestra tends to be very rigid. Before I stopped playing in 1953, I played fifty to sixty concerts a year, and one of the reasons I retired from concertizing was the rigorous concert schedule and playing the same concerto on Tuesday, Friday, and then again on Saturday. By Saturday, I would be bored to death playing the same thing. Arturo Toscanini stopped conducting regularly for the same reason. He had to do four concerts in four days. You just can't exist like that. You become an automaton. Perhaps one of the reasons I prefer recitals is that, when you play alone, you have to do it *all* alone. It is much easier to play with orchestra because your conductor is your spirit, your mind, and your means. When you play alone, it is more difficult, and I like to do things which are more difficult. Although the public likes to hear a soloist with orchestra because it is more glamorous, I like to play alone.

Then there is the traveling. When I used to tour, I took the train. I didn't sleep well, I didn't eat well. I didn't even like the train. Four concerts a week and traveling on the train were just too much. I suddenly felt very tired and decided to take a year off. Then, you see, I enjoyed the peaceful life so much, I kept taking year after year off.

But then the stories began circulating that you had gone mad, or that you were in an institution. What about these stories, are they a fact or fiction?

I guess human nature is prone to respond more to bad news rather than good news. Anyhow, in those twelve years I made seven recordings, so I guess I couldn't have been mad if I did that.

Two things happened which influenced me to return to the concert stage, however: I became tired of playing in the studio, and I realized that time had slipped by and if I were ever going to concertize again, the time was now. Today the flying doesn't tire me so much as sitting on the train did, although I don't enjoy traveling by plane for more than two hours. I like to stay where I have a kitchen, so that I can have my food prepared the way I like it. And I enjoy taking long walks each day when the weather permits and I allow myself only two cigarettes a day. As far as practicing is concerned, I usually try to do one to two hours a day. It isn't good to practice too much or your playing becomes too mechanical.

It is true that your transport your own piano for the concerts you play?

Usually, yes. It's a twenty-year-old Steinway which is shipped to each city while I'm on tour. I like to use my own piano for concerts. All pianos are more or less good, but they need constant care and don't often receive it. At least every month or two they should be tuned and voiced. If this isn't done, within a year's time the piano will run down like a human being who neglects his health. Pianos change their timbre and tone with the weather, the atmospheric conditions, or movement. When they come from the factory, they are like a new car. You can't drive them at top speed. There's even a difference in pianos from different areas. For instance the German Steinway differs from the American Steinway. And you should never mix them. The German wood cannot tolerate much change in the climate, so it starts to lose its voicing. European felt is different, too. A piano has some eleven thousand parts and, it one of those goes awry, then the piano doesn't function right. A piano is very vulnerable. Generally winters are too dry and summers too wet. I have my piano tuned once a month when I am at home, whether I play it or not.

I've even had a truck with two pianos on it following me. One of the pianos was my own for a recital, the other the new Steinway for the performance of the Rachmaninoff's Third Piano Concerto which I played for my fiftieth-anniversary celebrations in 1978. I chose this particular work for sentimental reasons.

Rachmaninoff was a great friend of mine. In fact, he was one of the greatest inspirations in my life. And so I indicated numerous times that, if I ever played a concerto, I would play that work. At first, that concerto didn't have any success, really. The reason was that audiences then were not as sophisticated as they are now. Then, too, I think Rachmaninoff became a little bit discouraged generally about public reaction to his works. He thought his works were good but that the people didn't understand them. He understandably became a little bitter. A young lady once asked him what inspired him to write such a beautiful work as the Second Concerto, which I think is brilliant, celebrated, and easy for the public to listen to. Rachmaninoff looked down at her from the top of his six-foot-four frame and replied gruffly, "Twenty-five rubles."

So he began to cut some of his works. The B-flat Sonata, for instance, is twenty-five pages longer in its first edition than it is in the second. Rachmaninoff thought it was too long and perhaps too complicated for pianists, so he decided to shorten it. I went to the master and told him, "I play the first version which is a beautiful thing, and then you do the second version which is even more difficult than the first. I protest!" Rachmaninoff was a very gloomy man and not very easy to approach, but we were fine friends. He replied, "Horowitz, go home. You're a good musician, so put it together and bring it to me. We'll see how it is." So I put it together, and he approved everything. I especially like the concerti of Rachmaninoff. The First I like very much; it is less played. The Second is played to death. The Fourth is the weakest. I think that his Rhapsody on a Theme by Paganini is a fine work. I recall when Rachmaninoff was composing it since I was in Switzerland at the time. He would call and tell me every time he had finished another variation. So it's rather obvious that he was one of the greatest inspirations in my life.

Rachmaninoff isn't the only composer I enjoyed playing, however. I delight in performing Chopin, and Schumann I greatly admire. As for Haydn, he is a genius. I also enjoy playing Debussy, and am fond of Scriabin because he is more of an expressionist. Scriabin has more meat. His music for the piano is very important, but when he touches the orchestra, in my opinion, he fails. His *Vers la flamme,* which he composed in 1914, has a certain mysticism about it. Debussy's music, on the other hand, is simply beautiful. I could easily see taking the orchestral works of this composer and transcribing them for piano. It would be quite lovely, I think. I enjoy playing some of the Prokofieff works as well. I met him many years ago, and I remember him telling me to play his Third Piano Concerto rather than his Second. "Don't play the Second," he told me. "It has too many notes."

And when I play for myself, I play everything. But when I set up my recital programs, I try to have a contrast in styles and pieces from the various periods. And I try to include works that aren't heard all the time. Really, the solo piano repertoire contains much beautiful music, an enormous number of fine works rarely, if ever, played. For example, I played in one of my Chicago recitals a few years ago one of the most romantic sounding of the Clementi sonatas, Sonata in F-sharp Minor, Opus 26, No. 2. It is a very singing sonata and quite a beautiful work which has been rarely heard by the public. Today Clementi is known more as a teacher than a composer, but you will find that he is a skeleton in Beethoven's music. I believe that Clementi influenced Beethoven more than any other composer. There's no doubt about it; he was a very great musician, although he does have some sonatas which are not very interesting. Clementi also composed quite a number of symphonies, twenty-five or thirty, I think, but he burned them after learning of a letter Mozart wrote criticizing his writing efforts in this direction. It seems that he learned of this letter's existence and possible publication so, as a devotee of Mozart, he burned them. Certainly Mozart had more genius than Clementi. Why, Mozart even built a new piano and influenced what could actually be played on it. His concerti are works of genius, and his sonatas are lovely too, but some are not at all interesting. They are played anyway because they have a good signature.

What are your thoughts on some of the piano literature written in the twentieth century?

That's another story. Again, much of it has a percussive sound, and I am against using the piano in this way. Even some of the music of Bartók and Stravinsky is too percussive for me. It may be beautiful music, but I don't really care to play it. I can listen to it and enjoy it, though. I also find it difficult to comprehend how some pianists are able to cover the gamut of repertoire from Bach to ultracontemporary in such a short time. Surely it must be difficult to make this transition because a certain amount of Bartók may become mixed up with Chopin, and of course it doesn't belong there at all. So much contemporary piano music is often played with very little expression. You have to maintain its rhythm and life, and it is very difficult to go from that to a Chopin waltz. It is a real aesthetic change of gears. Nevertheless, some pianists seem to be able to capitalize on playing modern music without playing Chopin and Schumann, too. It's a question of personality. No one forces a pianist into a certain repertoire. That, one must decide for himself.

Besides the freedom that must be granted the artist in matters of repertoire and interpretation, Horowitz believes that the virtuoso must be free to a certain extent of the influence of his own work. He has strong feelings about listening to his own recordings.

I never listen to my own recordings because I don't want to influence myself. As I said earlier, each time I play it is different. The great danger in listening to records is imitation. When Chopin taught and his pupils tried to imitate him, he sent them home and told them to bring something of their own.

So many times people who are studying piano study with recordings, and they are so used to hearing note-perfect performances on record that they want to duplicate the same note-perfect performance in the concert hall. They are not concerned about projecting the spirit of the music because they are concentrating so much on the notes; it becomes an obsession with them. If they make a smudge or something, they think it is a bad performance. A few wrong notes are not a crime. As Toscanini once said, "For false notes, no one was ever put in jail." As I said earlier, imitation is a caricature. It is better not to listen to yourself. Find your own way each time.

I grant you, though, that for some people imitation is a vehicle to discover themselves. As you seek to know, for instance, how Rachmaninoff created a work and do so by a synthesis, even if you do it differently, you are using his concepts to solidify your own concepts. But that is inspiration, too. I played the Rachmaninoff Third Concerto differently from the way he played it. And he agreed with my interpretation, because I was in the muse of composition; I felt from the inside what he wanted to say. I felt the atmosphere of the beginning of the nineteenth century in Russia at that time. I felt the pessimism of the Russians because of the deprivation, both intellectual and physical, like a feudal society. I tried to put all this into my playing.

I also remember when I recorded the Schumann Fantasy in 1965; if I listened to it today, it would bother me. An artist isn't the same day after day, so there can never be a *final* interpretation. It will be changing always. If I made four recordings of the same piece within a month, each would be different. I am not an assembly-line pianist. With recordings today, it is mechanically possible to do what I worked and sweated so many years to develop. So I do not allow the tone quality in my recordings to be altered or changed. If I make a mistake, I will do it over, but nothing I do can be touched. Recordings are like photographs: Sometimes you recognize the person and sometimes you don't. That's what happens very often in recordings.

Because of his vast experience as a virtuoso and his work with composers on their own compositions, the matter of Horowitz's own attempts at composing was quickly disposed of.

I composed many pieces I could play and even attain success playing them, but I don't do it. I played some of them for Prokofieff and for Medtner; Rachmaninoff was impressed with my compositions because they were similar to his in style. But you have to have ample background in composition and develop yourself, and I didn't, so I don't play my own works. If you are a composer, it is like becoming a painter. You can't start from the last year of Picasso. You have to start from the first years of Picasso and then become your own modern period. If you start from the last period, where do you go then? Moreover, you must be thoroughly versed in the style of the instruments. That's very important. There are good composers now, but they don't know the instruments; then there are also good composers who orchestrate beautifully, but there is not much substance to their music.

Yes, I am a composer, but a frustrated one. I transcribed as much music as you can think of for recording. But I don't remember one thing I did; I didn't even write some of it out. It is difficult today to be a successful pianist and compose. I somewhat neglected the study of counterpoint and things like that because I didn't have time. My father was a very prominent engineer from a bourgeois family in Russia. After the Communist revolution, he lost everything in twenty-four hours; I was only sixteen or seventeen at the time, but I felt it was now my time to help our parents because they had helped us. So I started to play concerts. Almost immediately, I had successful performances in Kiev, Moscow, and Leningrad. Now I am here, and I never caught up on the background.

I found that teaching has its own demands, too. In a way, it's like being a conductor who has to teach the orchestra how to play. Toscanini was exceptional in that regard. He knew how to play every instrument. He could tell the flute player how to blow and the cellist how to put his finger on the cello. He was exceptional. But in teaching you have to give so much of yourself. When I did some teaching, a session lasted not one hour, but three. I was so exhausted that I couldn't teach anymore. You also have to take a student who is eight or ten years old and educate him until he is twenty or twenty-two. If you take someone older, he thinks he knows more than the teacher, so you cannot shape him. And to teach children, I have not enough patience. Once in a while I listen to young pianists, but not too often because I don't attend concerts that frequently. Some time ago, though, I heard one new artist because he came to New York to visit me. We spent a few hours together, and he played for me. I had been told that he was a wonderful pianist so I listened, but I wasn't really that impressed. There seems to be an element of sameness in many pianists today. It is difficult at times to distinguish one pianist from the other. I think that perhaps it might be attributed to recordings and to teaching, too. Part of the education should be to learn to teach yourself. I think that a large part of the problem in this country is that people are taught how to be taught by someone else, but they are not taught how to be their own teachers. The conductor of an orchestra doesn't show the clarinetist how to play his instrument; he talks to him, tells him. When I taught, I very seldom went to the piano and told the student to play this way because that way is wrong. He must learn to figure it out for himself. The secret is not to force your personality on your student.

Today, musicians, at least some of them, want to do everything at once. Of course, youth is more interested in music today, but I think less committed to an ideal. George Szell once said that there's a lot of piano playing, but not enough music making.

Another element that is capable of hurting the artist is the competitions. From a managerial standpoint, it helps to capitalize, to have a winner, and then launch a career. But from the musical point of view, I don't like them because they select not by excellence, but by elimination. There was a big competition at the end of the nineteenth century, I believe it was the Anton Rubinstein Competition in Moscow. Busoni played and took third prize; first prize was won by Mr. Heinz. Do you know who Busoni is? Do you know who Heinz is?

The artist himself must do the launching of his own career. He has to prove what he can do for himself. You play a concert; you go into a second. In other words, you keep playing. Then the reputation develops and grows. I have never been in a competition in my life. I played some of my earliest concerts to almost empty halls at first, but then with each concert the halls became fuller and fuller. It's much better that way. When you win a competition, you're known, and much is expected of you right away. The other route allows you to grow and develop a reputation. That was my experience and it has been a highly rewarding one.

Byron Janis

BYRON JANIS

I III II III II III II III II III II III II III II III II I

Byron Janis and his wife Maria live on the top floor of a luxury
Park Avenue high-rise in Manhattan. The living room, where the
artist and I would talk for the next few hours, is just off the entrance
foyer. It looks like a room very much lived in, with an almost planned
careless attention paid to decor. An animal rug is strewn over the
carpet, and a huge sofa with billowy pillows possesses the room.
Pushed into the corner, where there is a huge bookcase filled with
books, music tape recorders, tapes and records, are two giant black
grand pianos, one a Steinway and the other a Baldwin. Mineral
specimens cover the coffee table and end tables adjacent to the sofa.
Mr. and Mrs. Janis are avid rock collectors, although they do not
like to be branded as "collectors" of any sort. They merely enjoy
owning this collection for the sense of beauty it gives them. The room
emits an aura of artiness as well as the feeling that it really is
"home." Double doors separate the living room from the rest of the
apartment so that we were entirely alone for our chat except once
when Mrs. Janis walked in with some newly sketched canvases and
waved hello to us. Maria, daughter of the late Gary Cooper, has
been a painter most of her life and exhibits her work frequently with
much success.

During the entire conversation, Janis sat in a straight-backed easy
chair. Generally, he kept his hands folded, but now and then he ges-
tured with his hands and arms, and frequently he smoothed back his

dark and longish strands of hair. He kept his legs crossed, every so often changing the crossing position. He was a most thoughtful conversationalist, occasionally looking upward to the high ceiling of the room as if to find a chronology of events written there.

He is a gentle-mannered man who speaks rather softly and punctuates his conversation with a nervous, light-hearted laughter. Words seem to come easily to him, and his fluidity was interlaced with bits of humor as he detailed his introduction to music and his early experiences with that art.

WHENEVER one shows a talent at a very early age, as in my case, the feeling is that music has chosen you. Unlike many other artists, I did not come from a background of parents who were musicians. My mother liked music very much, however, and as a young girl coming from Russia and working in the United States, she attended musical performances as time and money would allow. Nor was my father a musician. He was a businessman who possessed one of the most emotional and sensitive temperaments I have known. Therefore, once my musical talent was evident, both parents gave me all the encouragement they could. But it was an uncle of mine who unknowingly launched me into music. When I was five, he gave me a xylophone as a Christmas present. After the holidays, my kindergarten teachers told us to bring our favorite new Christmas toy to school. Out of quite a few toys, I chose the xylophone and dutifully carried it to school. During a play period, one of the teachers began playing the piano, and soon the children started to dance. Instead of dancing, I played my xylophone, following the exact tune she was playing on the piano. First I remember she was a little startled because she stopped playing. Then she took me by my hand and led me to the piano bench, sat me down and asked whether or not I thought I could do that on a piano. I said I would try, and again by ear I played the same little piece on the piano that she had been playing. What seemed so astonishing to her, somehow seemed natural to me. While I repeated the tune, she wrote something on a piece of paper, folded it, and pinned it to one of my suspenders. I was petrified at the thought of going home with that note for fear of what was written on it! I never did find out its content, but I do remember a flurry of excitement around the house after my mother had read it. A day or so later, both kindergarten teachers came to our home and explained what I had done. They had concluded that I had an extraordinary ear for music and that my parents ought definitely to start me studying an instrument. Because we had a piano at home, as did many homes (which probably accounts for there being so many more professional pianists in the world than other instrumentalists), I started studying.

My sister Thelma, who was several years older than I, had already begun studying piano at home. I remember, after the school incident, paying more attention to her practicing. I knew immediately when she struck a wrong note, so I would yell "wrong note" from some nearby room—which didn't exactly increase my popularity with her, but did sharpen my musical awareness! Then came the serious business of getting me started. Since we lived in Pittsburgh, it was decided that I should begin with a local teacher. The choice was Abraham Litow, quite an extraordinary man in his own way. He had a very strange method of teaching me. He wrote music out in letters combined with certain symbols which showed in which octave the note was to be played. I have no idea why he did it, but through this unusual musical code, I was learning to play the piano. I still have some of the pieces just as he wrote them out for me, which I now find quite baffling. In fact, I am unable to read one "note" of them.

Litow was also a severe taskmaster; every time I did something wrong, he cracked me on the hand or wrist with a ruler or pointer. Many a tear flowed from those whacks. Anyhow, his system seemed to work. I didn't realize how well until I had to substitute at a radio broadcast for one of his pupils who became ill. He said that I was ready, even though I had been playing for only six months, so I played Bach's *Solfeggietto*.

When I was about seven and a half years old, Mr. Litow told my parents and me that he had taken me as far as he could. He recommended that I play for Joseph and Rosina Lhevinne. He made the arrangements, so off we went, the family and I, to New York, where indeed I played for them. They said they definitely wanted to work with me and that I should come to New York to study as soon as possible. So my mother, my sister and I moved to New York, leaving my father in Pittsburgh to look after his business.

Then began one of the most wonderful but hectic and confusing periods of my life. Working with both the Lhevinnes simultaneously was surely an unusual and incredible experience—especially at that tender age. They were both great artists and teachers, as well as being husband and wife, and to expect total agreement between them would be quite unrealistic in either instance! Such was the case, at least, in the area of music. One incident that comes to my mind happened during a session with Madame Lhevinne. She was working on my hand position and fingering when in walked Joseph. "Why are you telling him that, Rosina? His hand is different from yours." Such disagreements confused and rattled me, but only momentarily; as I learned at that early age, there was not "one way." I shall never forget another time when Mr. Lhevinne was trying to impart a certain musical mood to me (I was eight years old at the time) by getting down on all fours and slowly crawling around the room. And from time to time he would take my hand off the piano, there would be a fifteen-second silence, accompanied by a facial grimace, a small legato purring sound would come from his throat, and then he would put my hand slowly back on the piano and say simply "try again." On one of these occasions, Mrs. Lhevinne walked into the room and he said to her, "Rosina, I don't think he understands me!" And, I must confess, at those moments, I didn't!

Since the Lhevinnes traveled a great deal and I needed regular supervision, it was decided after a year or so that I should study with someone else. However, I was to play for the Lhevinnes every month for a "progress check." The teacher I was sent to was Dorothea Anderson La Follete, who was incidentally also teaching Willie Kapell at the time, and who had studied with the Lhevinnes and knew something of their methods. For about eight months we worked together. Then she hinted that she felt I had no need to play for the Lhevinnes periodically and that I should work only with her. Her hint became almost an ultimatum: I had to work with her, exclusively, or she could give me no more of her time. My mother was, of course, deeply disturbed by all this as we wished to stay under the influence of the Lhevinnes. After talking to them about it, she was told to forget about such an arrangement. We would find another teacher. So at the age of ten, I was brought to Adele Marcus, who was not only an extraordinary pianist but an extraordinary teacher as well, and was doing some associate teaching for the Lhevinnes. For a year or so I studied under Miss Marcus, still playing occasionally for the Lhevinnes. Eventually I stopped playing for them and just worked with Marcus until I was sixteen. I took an average of two lessons a week for the six years of study with her, which really laid the foundations of my musical technique and thought. Though she was extremely detailed in her remarks and criticisms of my work, I felt somehow that it was still I who was expressing myself. I was never put into any one style or method of playing. Through the normal trials of musical growth, her total belief in me was a powerful asset to my musical development. Along with my musical studies, I was attending school for my standard education, but it was a private school, Columbia Grammar, in New York. They were most helpful by giving me a scholarship (we could not have afforded the tuition) and a special schedule to allow for my four hours of practice each day. Suddenly Miss Marcus decided to leave New York to join her husband, Fritz Kitzinger, also a noted musician, who had taken a teaching position in Texas.

To backtrack a bit now, when I was ten, I was taken by Miss Marcus to a school on the lower east side of New York called the Chatham Square Music School. It was founded by Samuel Chotzinoff, a man who played a tremendously important role in my life, as a musical mentor and also a very strong paternal figure to me. Mr. Chotzinoff was an extraordinary man of music and, as a pianist, accompanied Efrem Zimbalist, Heifetz and other great artists. Later, he became one of the leading music critics in New York. Then he was given the position as director of the National Broadcasting Company. And it was "Chotzi," as he was lovingly called by his friends, who persuaded Arturo Toscanini to come to the United States to conduct the NBC Symphony, which was formed for him by David Sarnoff and Samuel Chotzinoff. Little did I realize that, after playing for Chotzinoff at the age of ten, I would now have a second "family" in my life. He was married to Pauline Heifetz, who was the sister of Jascha Heifetz; they had two children, Blair and Ann. I not only lived with them in New York at one point, but spent many, many hours in their country house on weekends in the most stimulating of atmospheres—musical, literary and otherwise.

But to get back to our first meeting. Chotzi immediately arranged financial help for me, as my family had very little means. If it were not for the great generosity of Mary and William Rosenwald, my life would have been much more difficult indeed. They helped pay for my lessons and gave me monthly allowances for a period of time to come until I was able to support myself. I received my harmony and composition training at the Chatham School. Some of the composition lessons were with Roger Sessions, the noted composer. When Miss Marcus moved to Texas, it was Chotzi who advised me to continue my studies with her, as he found her such a superb teacher and everything had been progressing so well. And that is exactly what I did. In the meantime, my mother and sister returned to Pittsburgh to join my father. It was Jan Peerce who arranged a home for me in Dallas with some very close friends of his, Mr. and Mrs. Samuel Tallal. They were most kind to me during the two winters I spent with them. I shall never forget my first night away from home though. I wept the night through. But somehow the next day all traces of homesickness seemed to be gone and I was a very happy young man in my new setting.

From the age of fourteen to sixteen, Janis spent the winters in Texas and divided his summers between New York and Pittsburgh, visiting his family. It was during the winter of 1942, in Pittsburgh, that his career took another turn.

On a Sunday afternoon, I was scheduled to play the Rachmaninoff Second Concerto with the Pittsburgh Symphony Orchestra. I was sixteen at the time, and the conductor, Lorin Maazel, was fifteen. Vladimir Horowitz had played a recital on Saturday night, and his train

Eugene Ormandy presenting a birthday cake to Byron Janis on his twenty-first birthday

wouldn't leave until Sunday night. Although I wasn't aware of it, the manager of the concert asked him whether he might like to hear a young pianist play Rachmaninoff. Out of curiosity, I suppose, Horowitz came. When I had finished and was standing backstage, Horowitz came over to me and simply said, "Good." When I had recovered from my surprise, he confessed that he had enjoyed the performance very much, and inquired when I might be going to New York. I remember saying that I didn't know, because I was still living and studying in Texas with Miss Marcus. He urged me to call him as soon as I arrived in New York because he wanted to hear me play more and talk with me. Then he left to catch his train and left me in an imaginable state of high excitement.

His invitation kept popping into my mind all during the following winter and, when spring arrived, I returned to New York. Naturally I called Horowitz, and he invited me to his apartment and asked me to play whatever I wished for him. I remember I chose the G Minor Sonata of Schumann, among other works. After talking a bit, he told me he would like me to work with him. He imposed certain conditions, however, on my studying with him, especially that I would not play for other artists or teachers. He felt that they would confuse me because, during our period of study, there would be times when I might exaggerate or underplay something and, if I played at that moment for somebody close to me whose musical opinion I respected, they might say to me, "Oh, you're on the wrong track. It's too exaggerated, or it's not enough. You're going the wrong way." I think it was a very wise judgment on his part and an accurate one since I actually did play hooky once, playing for someone whose opinion I valued and who became quite upset upon hearing me. Naturally, that was most unsettling. I think what Horowitz was really trying to say was that, until you find your own way of saying something, just as in life, you're prone to overexaggerate one side or the other. I must admit that, at the time, his restrictions about my playing for others had me somewhat worried; but, as time went on, I learned to respect his feelings and I grew to understand more clearly what he had meant. So at the age of seventeen, I started working with Horowitz, becoming really his first pupil. We worked about once a week and the lessons would be anywhere from one to two hours. If something didn't go right, I remember he would say, "Well, something doesn't sound right. I think you should look at it some more and bring it back to me again." He would never try to interpret the work for me, even when he felt my performance of it lacked conviction and needed rethinking.

He was also most serious about the lessons being continuous.

Therefore, I joined him and Mrs. Horowitz on tour frequently to continue my studies. And although there were many musical evenings where he would play endlessly—those times I shall never forget—at the lessons, he never played a note for me. When I mentioned this to him, he explained that he had very strong feelings about the problems that came from imitation, especially problems in interpretation. A great pianist like Horowitz can show another pianist the possibilities and marvelous capabilities of the piano, the function of the pedals, technical effects, what to do to obtain color effects and an endless string of other particulars. But phrasing, the part of the piano that sings, the heart, the soul, the inner color, cannot be given from one artist to another.

In his own teaching, Janis practices some of these precepts which he believes are deeply important. At master classes and at his occasional private lessons, Janis rarely touches the piano.

I believe it absolutely defeats the purpose of teaching, a word much abused in today's pedagogy. If you're talking about "teaching" a nontalent, you're talking about something quite futile. I'm speaking of talent; talent needs a very limited amount of teaching and a very careful approach. Otherwise all you get is a mimic, and that's what will happen ninety-eight percent of the time when you demonstrate a point at the piano. There have been many talents, great talents, who studied with outstanding performing artists, and who simply became mimics and failed to flourish as they should. In no way am I saying the fault lies with the teacher alone. A strong teacher needs a strong pupil as a strong mother or father needs a strong child. Frequently, people with talent study too long and too late in life anyway. I stopped my studies with Horowitz when I was twenty. Actually, it was he who influenced my decision. "You'll go out and make mistakes," he said, "but that's okay; they'll be your mistakes. Let them be yours. Say something with your music; it doesn't matter what, but say something that's *you*."

You know, we pianists are really blessed, on the one hand, to have such an extraordinary instrument at our disposal, one that is capable of doing practically anything; and yet, on the other hand, it is really a percussion instrument that has to be made to sing. There is our great difficulty—to make a percussion instrument sing; however, it's really not that difficult to do if one thinks of the piano as a *singing* instrument that is capable of percussion. It's the one instrument in the world that is capable of singing and accompanying itself. The great endless fascination with the possibilities of the instrument is very exciting. What the *artist* does with that is another thing; but there is and should be a real joy in trying to uncover all the secrets of this extraordinary instrument. I look on it not only as a singing or percussion instrument, but one which is capable of making all kinds of orchestral effects as well. The piano has this marvelous capacity all within itself. Consequently, there isn't any need for electrical contrivances to make it sound like various instruments. And as a pianist, if you feel that you want it to sound like another instrument, it will. Take a piece that is obviously an extraordinary example of demonstrating the use of the piano orchestrally, namely, *Pictures at an Exhibition* by Mussorgsky. For such a long time, this piece had no success. My feeling is that not only was it difficult, but it was played as a piano piece rather than an orchestral piece on the piano. In other words, perhaps the pictures were being painted with watercolors instead of vibrant oils. Consider it, perhaps, in this light. It's as if the piano can reproduce images in miniature or on a larger canvas, even a whole tapestry. That piece of music is an entire mural. It's a huge, beautiful wall. But if you reduce its dimensions, it's simply not going to be successful. With a first-class piano there's a vast range of sound that you have at your disposal to make this piece sound as it should.

Certainly times have changed since the twenties when pianists like Anton Rubinstein, Hofmann, Rachmaninoff, and Paderewski traveled not only with their own pianos, but with their own tuners as well. Today, hardly a handful of pianists have their pianos accompany them, much less a tuner. Yet, I don't know whether people realize just how important that combination is to a performance, because really a piano is our voice and, if our voice is a little bit hoarse or muted or a little bit brash, there is very little we can do. At those times, we try many ways of compensating for the problem, but we can't always succeed.

Speaking of the twenties brings to mind a subject I'm very impassioned about, namely, romanticism in music. I'm afraid we like to pigeon-hole things in the world, that is, to categorize them into one area or another, probably because it's easier for us to conceive of them in this way. But, in doing so, we do ourselves and others, I believe, a great injustice. There is usually a word which describes this categorizing which becomes extremely perverted and changes the essence of its meaning. Such is the case in speaking of the word *romantic*. We have a period in music which we categorize as the romantic period. Yet, surely romance has existed since the world's inception; and romantic music has existed since the inception of music. *All* music is romantic. All great music speaks from the heart. But what I think happens is that sometimes we have vogues or fashions that stay with us for a time and then disappear. Unfortunately, the "good" goes out of fashion as well as the less desirable. The "anti-romantic" movement in the world was not really directed against romance, although it seemed to be. I believe it came about because of the *excesses* in romantic playing, that is, when it is no longer from the heart, but from the mind. Whenever you get extremes like that, somebody will always come along and want to destroy not only that extreme, but in the process destroys both consciously or unconsciously the *true* essence of music. For me, of course, this is an incredible idea. How can one take the heart out of music? How can one take the heart out of romance? How can one take the heart out of life? I have the feeling that the pendulum is swinging back, as it always does. It is swinging back to a feeling that romance is not such a bad thing after all. I've noticed it in the playing of some of the younger pianists; and I've also noticed it in their attitudes. What causes this return, I don't know. Perhaps it is this extraordinary age of technology which seems to leave the heart out of everything. Experimentation and discovery in music must continue, but not at the expense of art.

Music is still more than singing from the depths of the soul. Music *is* the soul. I think Chopin put it pretty well when he instructed his students to "play with all your soul, *all* your soul." This is what you have to do if you want to make really great music. As in life, the more of yourself you give to others, the more you usually will receive in return. I say "usually" because there are people who seem frightened (I thought of saying incapable, but I believe the correct word is *frightened*) to give all and conversely those who somehow find it frightening when all is given to them. But, for me, that is the only way. Only then can music evoke fully the beauties and mysteries of this world and other worlds we don't comprehend. It's those moments of magic when the soul is fully singing, and the technique and the imagination are all working in conjunction; *then* something happens. Call it "inspiration," call it "catching the elusive now," call it whatever you like, but that's music. There's no piano, no pianist; it transcends both piano and pianist.

I have always been challenged by all music, to capture all different styles. To try to really know the man, his background, his thoughts and feelings (his own letters are the best guide for this) is perhaps the best way to understand and re-create his music. That's what makes a re-creative artist's life a creative one. What happens when you play a recital consisting of Mozart, Chopin, Debussy, Prokofieff? You're playing music of four entirely different men, from entirely different backgrounds, entirely different styles and periods. It's like being an actor coming out on the stage, playing four entirely different roles. You're trying to re-create the essence of Mozart, the essence of Chopin, the essence of Debussy, the essence of Prokofieff. That's the great challenge of being an artist; to delve deeply into, or to put it another way, to quietly step aside allowing yourself to be a channel letting your talent merge with that of the creator and his creation. And of course there is the ever-important ingredient—the audience, the listener. The listener must also include the artist himself.

Putting philosophical thoughts and ideas on music and pianism aside, what would Janis seek to find if it were possible to go back in time, and where would he like to have been?

Of all the eras in the past, the nineteenth century fascinates me most. And I would like to have lived in Paris. Paris at that time was the center of intense artistic activity. Artists were intellectually and emotionally alive; they worked together, even though they represented all different forms of creativity. In spite of my great abhorrence for comparisons, Paris just happens to be my favorite city in the world; I always feel that there is a beauty there that cannot be equaled anywhere else. The shadows of the past seem to haunt me more there than anyplace else. Especially I would like to have met Chopin. Ever since I was very young, I found myself reading, devouring all the literature I could find about him. And my interest wasn't just in Chopin, the composer and pianist; it was in Chopin the man. As I continued to learn more about him, especially through his letters, I realized that the man was as intriguing to me as the composer. There seems to have been some kind of thread of Chopin running through my life starting with my chance encounter at Nohant in 1955 with Aurore Lauth Sand, granddaughter of George Sand, and continuing through my discovery of four manuscripts in Chopin's hand and the film I made on his life—a one-hour portrait that French television coproduced. I was visiting Nohant with my first wife shortly after the birth of my son Stefan, just to get the feeling about that extraordinary place where not only Chopin, but so many artists spent so much time and had done so much work. Conversing as I did with Madame Sand was rather like being back in the nineteenth century, as she lived totally in the past. She told me that she was eleven when her grandmother died and she was so profoundly impressed by her grandmother that she decided to dedicate her entire life to her memory, which she did. She told me many tales of her father Maurice, who was George Sand's son. Some of these concerning Chopin were extraordinarily moving and fascinating. It was truly like being there. That day lives very strongly in my memory. Curiously enough, it was the first time I ever played in France, and it was for Aurore at Nohant. She had a little piano which was closed and locked. She opened it shortly before we were departing and asked me if I wouldn't play something for her. I played the Nocturne in D-flat Major of Chopin and a sonnet, the *Sonnetto 104 del Petrarca* of Liszt. You can imagine what a moving experience it was for me to play for her in that setting.

The thought of the Chopin-Sand relationship and the disparity of their careers prompted me to ask whether there was any conflict in having a wife with such strong interests of her own alongside of music.

Having separate careers and still being as one is not difficult when one is married to Maria, who is not only an extraordinary wife, but has a strong talent and life of her own. She is a painter by profession and has had many very successful exhibits. She also does research in the field of parapsychology, and with all this still manages to put her life with me first. She travels with me on almost every tour and we have a marvelous time together. Practically speaking, she also takes care of many details that save me much time and, most important, has a strongly instinctive musical sensitivity. Perhaps most women would find such a life most trying. But, though music is the center of my life, she can participate in many ways in that music. For many other professional men, that could not be the case. So perhaps there are some rewards in being married to a musician!

Despite his allegiance to music, Byron Janis doesn't limit his acquaintances to musicians. The Janises' social life at home consists of small dinner parties of guests who comprise a wide spectrum of interests. "All things in life interest me," he says. "Sometimes you find music in the least likely places!" Otherwise, what free time he has he uses to read, write—among other things, popular music—and jot down the "improvisations I just sit down and play." He considers it tragic that we don't continue improvisations as part of our musical culture.

It's a great art form when done either in private or public. And it should be encouraged. Much of the outstanding music we hear, many of the formal works of Beethoven, can't really compare with some of his improvisations we are told by musicians who heard them. When they are good it is because they are spontaneous, because they are free-spirited. There are no "retakes." The results can be something very special.

They are also from the heart and from the soul, and that is all Byron Janis asks of any music from any musician.

Lili Kraus

LILI KRAUS

▌▐▐▌ ▐▌ ▐▐▌ ▐▌ ▐▐▌ ▐▌ ▐▐▌ ▐▌ ▐▐▌ ▐▌ ▐▐▌ ▐▌ ▐▐▌ ▐▌ ▐

Resplendent in a gray and lilac pants suit, a smiling Lili Kraus opened the door of her suite at the Mayflower Hotel in New York. Her graying hair was piled up in a crown which accentuated the beautiful features and angular lines of her face. The glowing eyes, the warmth and easiness of the smile, along with her effervescent charm and manner, would make anyone feel at ease in her company. After initial greetings, she abruptly suggested a trip to the coffee shop to pick up sandwiches, coffee and ice cream to fortify ourselves against the several hours ahead. Carefully balancing coffee, ham sandwiches and vanilla ice cream, we returned to her apartment where, between bites of food and sips of coffee, Madame Kraus began reminiscing about her life, particularly the influence her imprisonment by the Japanese had on her outlook and her playing. Assuredly, the years in prison had been an overwhelming experience, so complex that it would be almost impossible to refer to it in every aspect.

NOBODY can answer that, my friend, in the brevity of time and space at our disposal. I suppose the most recognizable trait that stands out though, is that, without those experiences, I would never have achieved the depths of compassion and, on the other hand, the

appreciation of the richness of life that fills my soul and spirit ever
since liberation, to this day. *Depth* may not be the right word either;
perhaps *immediate* or *irresistible* come closer to my meaning. The
immediate appreciation of the sandwich I just ate; the spontaneous
gratitude for having a clean cup like the one I'm holding; and the
countless other wonders, considered trivial, could never, never have
grown to the degree of gratitude and enthusiasm with which they now
occur. Indeed, gratitude and enthusiasm rule my life as they do my
performances; they appear in my teaching; and they trigger my understanding of the composers—I give them all I have and thank them
with all I am for the privilege of being their interpreter.

It seems to me that my happiness at any given performance is easily understandable, seeing that, for four years, I played no music at
all, piano or anything else. I didn't even have the opportunity to look
at a composer's score from 1942 until 1945. We were in Djakarta on
a concert tour in 1940. No one expected the Japanese to occupy Java
(Indonesia today)—without a base in the vicinity—but they did. In a
sense, though, we were prisoners in Djakarta before our actual incar-
ceration. The *Anschluss* (annexation of Austria) degraded and diminished civilized Austria into the state of a German provincial police
district thanks to Hitler's brutal "conquest." Even though my husband, the late Dr. Otto Mandl, was Austrian, it was impossible for us
to return to Austria for various reasons. First, my husband was part
Jewish; second, all Austrians, living at home or abroad—in our case
in Italy—were to exchange their passports, thereby becoming Germans automatically. The Hitler-Mussolini alliance made Italians "de-
pendents" of Germany; therefore, the *questura* in Milan wrote us letter after letter urging us to exchange our passports. Finally, my
husband indicated that we would become British citizens and it then
would serve no purpose to have German papers for the short interim
period. In fact, in 1939, we obtained British "Certificates of Iden-
tity." We were fortunate in this respect, otherwise we would have
been caught in a cage. On behalf of the German government, we
were expelled from Italy, where we had lived for eight years. The
countless treasures we had were left behind—among them, two Stein-

way concert grands, facsimiles of Leonardo da Vinci's diaries, three thousand books, many of them first editions—and they fell into the hands of Germans. Our 450-year-old manor house, which was originally built for a Hapsburg, was also lost. Today, this splendid house is a protected national treasure of Italy.

In the course of a lifelong friendship, my husband translated and edited all of H. G. Wells's works, including his last work, *Shape of Things to Come,* wherein Hitler was described as a gangster. And this was a reason for not remaining in Italy and certainly another reason for not returning to Austria.

After fleeing from Italy in 1938, we found ourselves in Paris for a short time. From there we traveled to London, where we met, once again, the Honorable Walter Nash, then Minister of Finance and Immigration in New Zealand. Nash was an intimate friend of Wells and also a good friend of ours. He proposed that we become New Zealand citizens. In fact, he even wrote to the British Foreign Office requesting that we be given traveling papers until New Zealand passports could be obtained at the earliest possible moment after our arrival. However, before we could reach "our promised land," a concert tour obligation had to be fulfilled in the Dutch East Indies via Hong Kong, Singapore and then Djakarta.

After the Japanese occupation of Djakarta, following the fall of Singapore, no one bothered us too much for a while because the area was composed of a mixture of Japanese, Dutch and Australians. It was rather difficult to keep track of just who was who and what was what. Nevertheless, we knew we couldn't leave so, to avoid the stifling heat in the city, we rented a house in the mountains where it was cooler. Meanwhile, I had enjoyed a profound, warm and happy friendship with the American-born wife of the Dutch governor-general. On account of our friendship, I was arrested by the military secret police. It seems that a Dutch woman was in trouble because of a liaison with a Japanese officer and, as a result, was severely beaten. She was promised freedom from further beatings if she would sign a charge against the two of us. The charge, false of course, was that we had conspired to liberate the handful of British and Australian pris-

At her home in Brownsville, North Carolina, Lili Kraus plays songs for her daughter Ruth Pope, son-in-law Dr. Fergus Pope, and their children, *left to right,* Frances, Daniel, and Clara.

oners to kill the guards and set all prisoners free. It was really a farfetched "cock-and-bull" story. Of course, we were arrested and sent to a prison in Djakarta.

Because the children were with us, everyone suggested that my husband go to the rented house and stay as far from the city as he could for as long as he could. But he didn't! He just couldn't tear himself away from me, knowing I was down there in the "inferno"—the infamous subterranean prison cells of the secret police.

For four days, he came time after time to the prison, begging them to take him instead of me. He told them he'd assume the charge since I was only an artist and a mother and completely apolitical. At first, they absolutely refused to listen to such an exchange; later, someone in the high command thought it might be possible, but it never worked out. They arrested my husband, too. I suppose they did so to be on the safe side. Of course, I did not know that he had walked in there on his own but, because he had done so, they let him pass my cell on the way to his own so that he could speak to me and see that I had not been badly treated. And just to let him know that I was all right, I began to sing. I was ordered to be quiet since even talking was forbidden. I was threatened with a beating but, ten minutes later, I began to sing again. The beating never came, and my husband gave up counting after I had sung a thousand Hungarian songs.

I realized that, in a sense, they had to leave me alone. They could kill me, but that would have been too difficult to explain. Least of all could they beat or torture me, because they knew who I was and were probably afraid that, if I were physically harmed, I'd tell the world all that happened in the course of my travels. I did have one fear, though, and it was that they might violate or mishandle me. But they let me alone. In fact, you might say they behaved extremely well, considering what they really could have done. After all, we were entirely at their mercy.

At the beginning, I guess I was just too dazed to think or feel anything. I never became used to the yelling and cries of pain that echoed through those subterranean cells. I would sit with my hands over my ears to help shut out the screams. I imagined that Dante's Inferno was a tea party compared to this place. Then, when my husband was imprisoned, as I told you, I began the singing, so I had little time to think of myself. Occasionally, though, I did take a long, wistful look at my hands and wondered what might become of them. But the hands did not suffer. On the contrary, my hands became so superb *because* I did the forced labor after being moved to a POW camp, although the other women in the prison offered, with sincere generosity, to take over my duties. Obviously, I couldn't possibly accept any such sacrifices on their part. As long as I was there with them, I felt compelled to do my share. Besides, if the good Lord wanted me to continue playing, play I would! Again, if this was the way He chose to tell me that my performing days were over, I was bound to stop—no matter what the reason. I did develop a painful shoulder because I had to straddle a well and pull buckets full of water to our level. In this particular prison, there were no faucets and so there wasn't any running water. About forty buckets had to be pulled up in the morning, forty at noon and forty in the evening. At the end of my first day of doing this, my finger joints were so swollen and so painful that I couldn't open the fingers. I was as frightened as I was shocked. But only for a moment, because the thought came again that, if I'm going to play the piano again, I will; and if it isn't meant to be, I won't! So I worked on. And as a consequence, my hands became wonderfully strong.

However, it wasn't the manual work or possible damage to my hands that bothered me so much. What really ate me up was the longing for my music and my family. I could never decide which anguish was more tormenting; however, I was consumed by the desire to sit down at the piano and play and play. This longing almost drove me mad. So I resorted to a kind of "recall" from the subconscious realizing that I had to materialize all the music within me—the composition and the projection—silently. I worked so hard at doing this that scores and technique, which seemed to have been buried many fathoms deep, now appeared so real, so present, that I knew that if I were seated before a piano I could play pieces I hadn't practiced since childhood, and in doing so discover new wonders that never seemed so apparent before.

Later, at another prison, when the Japanese brought in a piano at Christmas time, I was commanded, not asked, to play for the other prisoners. It was as if a crystal source had sprung up from the sand of the Sahara before a man who had spent days and days wandering in the desert; I just poured over that piano and, without any music, I played on and on with my whole heart, in pain and joy. I don't even remember how long, but I don't recall repeating any piece, nor do I remember making any mistakes while playing them. It was as if I could play anything and everything ever known to man—what merciful madness. It seemed all I had to do was make the effort to recall the piece. It was then, too, that I realized the strength of my fingers and that the forced labor had helped rather than hurt them.

I became more conscious of something else during this period of my life, namely, that an artist truly is *born* and not made. Talent is given, and there is no way it can be poured into someone. An individual can study until doomsday but, if the gift isn't there, progress will remain forever only surface brilliancy, technical progress at its best. What sustained me most in those years were my faith, my love and my identification with music. I was able to live in the music. And during this period, the conviction grew in me that, unless man totally disappears from the face of the earth, whether by atomic bombs or abuses of nature, his final evolution will be the replacement of words by music. Nobody will talk, nobody will sing. Music may well become the communication between man because it will be so alive in everybody that it will not need any more material manifestation. When you look at a person, you will know what kind of music is going on in him: "song without words," ultimately, in the final destination, "song without sound." Who knows?

Returning to the present, I also have some thoughts to share about concert performances, particularly what goes through my mind before I walk onstage. Imagine, I am so excited that I have the feeling of being so faint, so helpless, as if the very candle of my life is going to snuff out. I feel as if I couldn't lift an arm, move a finger, and as if I'd never seen a piano; it is as if I'm lost and don't know what to do. But when I walk out and see the friendly grin of those eighty-eight keys reassuring me, inviting me, I love them, and then everything falls into place. Whenever I perform, my happiness hangs on every note. Certainly there are times when I don't feel like playing but, once I'm on that stage, inspiration guides and lifts me.

I never eat anything before a performance because I believe that every fiber of your body has to serve the performance and you cannot burden your stomach by making your digestive juices work. If you do, you function too much in the stomach and not enough in the spirit and the brain.

During the performance, this person you see before you, this Lili

Kraus, ceases to exist as an individual. I exist only in the music I project to the audience. My mortality is eclipsed. I think one of the finest compliments I ever received came from my revered teacher, Artur Schnabel, when he said that he never knew anyone with so much joy in playing. I suppose that is why to me the worst agony in the world is the feeling that I've failed in projecting this joy. Failing God, the composer or myself, the artist—any of the three—I'm in abject misery. So it really isn't necessary to have a critic to tell me how I've done. I'm my worst, most merciless, demanding critic. Information from the past indicates that creative people have always had a dislike for critics, with a mixture of fear and contempt. I don't dislike them. If they hear something that genuinely pleases them, that's fine. And if they hear something they don't especially care for, that's all right, too. However, I do seriously question myself, in either case, as to what might have caused their critical listening to arrive at that particular conclusion; and there I might agree or disagree, enthusiastically or mildly, and all shades in between—but I am learning. Nevertheless, we have to admit that the critic is important because he can make or mar the career of an artist, at least temporarily.

After World War II, aspiring American pianists would travel to Europe to give recitals in hopes of receiving favorable reviews that would launch their careers at home. Generally, the European reviewers were more charitable, but their reviews didn't necessarily guarantee success. Furthermore, the differences between America and Europe have greatly leveled out now. Due to the accessibility and exchange of the media, namely, records and live performances on television and radio, the tradition of Europe is no longer so alive. Today, one of the primary routes to success is through the competitions because this is where the young artist is heard by experts in the field. I don't greatly love competitions, even though I'm frequently a judge at them. But we are fortunate that they have been invented, because it gives talented young artists an opportunity to further their careers. In my time, there was nothing like that at all: Each artist had to fight his way, step by step, to make a career. Now the youngsters can gain a foothold, *if* they have promising talent. And the competition toughens them. After all, the pianists who go through the competitions are excellent players, and they have to pit their own talent against that of their peers. It fascinates me, though, to see how kind they are to each other. In fact, it's one of the really great joys I experience from judging these competitions. Naturally, I'm happy to hear someone play a piece as I think it should be played, but the way they behave toward each other is wonderful to observe.

Their playing, however, at times amazes me. Technically, they are wonderful; after all, we are living in a technological epoch which was never dreamed of in our evolution. The emphasis, therefore, seems to be on playing every note in its proper place, but without making a personal statement, showing no passionate involvement and taking no risks. Sometimes, when I listen to them, I fail to detect any joy or sadness. It all sounds the same: slow, fast, soft, loud. But I want to hear concepts, not just notes. The emotional content of what is played must be in head and heart, not just in the fingers or on the sleeve. At the competitions, the young pianists are sometimes very wary of unmasking themselves. They play contemporary music magnificently, and do rather well with the virtuoso pieces. But when they reach farther back to Bach, Scarlatti, Mozart, Beethoven or even Schubert, they show little understanding of the composer's intent.

Many young pianists today are completely separated from the tradition of "classic" or even "romantic" feeling, and I don't see any road back for them because they are ceaselessly bombarded with noise that takes them further away. Consider for a moment the noise of the city, the road, the air, not to speak of jazz and rock music. Certainly jazz and rock have wonderful rhythms which are almost primitive in origin. Such rhythms hypnotize the mind, actually dull it, so that the listener is dazed. But the great masters do just the opposite: They stimulate and refresh the awareness of the spirit. As everyone knows, there are no depths of unhappiness, tragedy, frustration, anger, and despair that haven't touched Mozart, for instance, to the very core of his being; nor was there any nuance, any form of delight that passed him by. An inspired musician will wed his life to the essence of the piece, demonstrating the glow, the swiftly-changing visions through the symbols that were Mozart's language. Some of our young pianists don't seem to let all this shine through the notes of the score. It was Goethe who said that we go through periods of history which are stamped either by spirit or bear the sign of technical progress. But the times which will be remembered are the epochs of spiritual enlightenment, lifting mankind Godward—not the technical achievements, even if they should be beneficial and spectacular. It would do our youngsters good to have these thoughts instilled in them. There is far too much emphasis placed on technical matters. When I studied with Schnabel, he never taught technique; but he had the great gift of bringing to life music and all the potential that lay within the student. You can't imbue a student with a spirit he doesn't possess, but you can elucidate and develop what is there. Nor can you bend your music to your potential; you have to elevate your potential to the music. Too much work on technicalities simply kills the spirit, so we are never really introduced to the young pianist as a musician.

All of this, however, doesn't mean that, even for an instant, should we slacken in our technical endeavors: Without mastery, the artistic vision cannot be done justice. The piano is really a marvelous instrument. In a way it is not only the most sophisticated, but also the most transcendental of all instruments, because it forces you to rely not on technique only, as many would have it today, but on your creative imagination almost to the point of sorcery. The paradox lies in the fact that the voice of the piano dies in the moment of birth. Once you have struck the key, the sound can only diminish; there is no way of actually prolonging it. It is up to your imagination and vision to pretend and make believe that there is a continuity of sound equivalent to the sound of a flute, a voice, a cello, a horn, in fact, a whole orchestra. So the piano has all the richness imaginable besides the polyphony it can produce. But the orchestra, too, has to be transcended to convey the essence of the music; and so, the piano must also be transcended to produce a sound that is the sound of all sounds. Behind these sounds and through them the composer is able to relate his cosmic experience.

A good deal of what one can bring to music or obtain from it involves the total being. When I spoke of Mozart a few moments ago, I pointed out the gamut of his experiences. He is the divine genius who was able to express the deepest thoughts with the fewest words. One simply has to love Mozart. His grace, his sweetness, his humor were of a kind so unique that every effort to describe it in words has failed, even when the description came from the heart and mind of great writers or poets. His essence forever is ineffable like music itself; and it is only possible through God's grace alone, that some of the incomparable beauty of that music is revealed in a rare, blessed hour by the inspired artist.

Mozart has given this gift of sweetness, which is so extraordinary because it is born out of tragedy. I feel an affinity to Mozart because he, like myself, had an almost unbearable sensitivity for all suffering around him, if I dare to speak of myself in the same breath with his name. Now, to be able to bear the pain, the dear Lord gave us as an antidote a capacity for tremendous serenity, humor and gaiety which leads to happiness; otherwise one couldn't bear the suffering. There's an old saying that the sea is as deep as the mountain is high on its shore. Thus, if you know these extremes of happiness and unhappiness, you are able to face whatever comes your way. Mozart's music is so irresistibly lovable because he didn't, like Beethoven, fight for perfection of expression; his perfection was in implying the totality of life, the good and the bad of it.

In his diary, Leonardo da Vinci said that the true experience of the artist at times is so terrifying that, if the artistic vision were presented in full truth to the layman, he would be so shocked that he would flee in terror. Therefore, according to Leonardo, it is the duty and sacred privilege of the creative artist to cloak his experience in the garb of love and perfection. Now this is precisely what Mozart has done, and his music has become so much a part of me that I agonize when the music turns to the minor, and I'm redeemed when it reverts to the major. If I could go back to times past, I certainly would pay homage to Bach, Haydn and Beethoven, but I would most assuredly bow low and kneel in the presence of Mozart. And if I may see him someday in the hereafter, I hope that he will confide in me, saying that I have not altogether displeased him with my interpretations of his works.

Rosalyn Tureck

ROSALYN TURECK

Rosalyn Tureck lives in a high-rise apartment building in the center of Manhattan. The long foyer through which I walked to get to the living room is filled with books on subjects ranging from music to religion, psychology, sociology, and philosophy. Once in the living room, Alice, Ms. Tureck's general assistant for some twenty years, told me to relax for a few minutes because my hostess would be slightly detained.

Art pieces, paintings, Rembrandt etchings, Egyptian tapestries, wall hangings, and an array of African drums, string instruments, lyres, a lute and other antique European instruments decorated the living room. A bust of Ms. Tureck sculpted by Sir Jacob Epstein was perched on its pedestal adjacent to the large, black Steinway grand piano which had a Bach score lying open on its rack. Another section of the room contained an eight-foot concert harpsichord made by William Dowd of Cambridge, Massachusetts, and a clavichord by Robert Goble of Oxford, England. A glass table with gold casting and French eighteenth-century gold chairs stood several yards away. Next to it were drawers, boxes, and folders crammed with biographical and concert information obviously meant to be used to document the facts, theories, and opinions that would form the substance of the interview.

Rosalyn Tureck soon entered the room flashing a wide smile and apologizing for having kept me waiting. The green silk Chinese robe she wore covered a small figure which belies her photographs. She has piercing brown eyes, speaks with clear enunciation, and possesses a strong laugh. During our conversation, she resorted more to facial expressions than to arm or hand gestures. Between munching on cheese and sipping several cups of tea, brought out by Alice on Ms. Tureck's cue, the artist discussed her career development, particularly her pianistic studies as a child, the various competitions she had won, and of course her becoming a Bach specialist. She spoke fluently, referring frequently to the vast amount of printed matter that lay about us.

ALTHOUGH no musical career follows a stereotyped pattern, and my own can certainly attest to that, still a thread of similarity, usually an atmosphere of music, runs through most of them in the early stages. My two older sisters and an older cousin studied piano. As soon as school was over for the day, they rushed home and took turns practicing on our upright piano. Then there was my mother's singing. I think she had a great voice; she sang almost constantly. Even when I was outside playing, I could easily hear her powerful tones from half a block away. So I was constantly surrounded by music.

Then one day, at the age of four, I simply sat down at the piano and began to play. I didn't pounce on the keys, I didn't use a fist, nor did I pick out notes with one finger. I used both hands and played. For four years I played, somehow picking out the melodies and finding the harmonies. I remember that, by the time I was nine, the entire baseboard of the piano from the keyboard right down to the pedals was completely covered with dents and scratches, each one the result of a kick at my distress over not being able to find a note, a chord, or a harmony. I didn't read music, so I tried to play what I had heard from my sisters and from my mother's singing. I also improvised and composed continuously. But I sought to play music with both hands, because I thought of music in terms of a complete score rather than single melodies with an occasional harmonic chord.

When I was eight, I played for my sisters' teacher, and he took me on. He was to have the distinction of being the only teacher who took a fee for my lessons. I studied with him for a year at the end of which he entered me in a contest for young pianists in Chicago. The prize was a debut recital. I won the contest and so made my solo debut at age nine in the Lyon and Healy Hall before a full audience, including critics from the *Chicago Tribune* and the *Chicago Herald-Examiner.* Apparently everyone was satisfied with my efforts because three months later I played another complete program in a public recital.

Following the second recital, it was discovered that I wasn't quite sure of the difference between an eighth note and a half note. To this day I don't know by what intuition or talent or intellection I had been able to play the previous programs; but I did play them. I even accompanied my eldest sister in the Mendelssohn Concerto in G Minor; I played the orchestral accompaniment, most of it from memory. But by what faculties, I hardly know. I can only hazard a guess that my absolute pitch, with which I was born, and a coordinating mental facility were certain factors.

The quality of my first teacher may be ascertained by the following episode. At one of my sister's lessons he had her return repeatedly to a section where the indication "tenuto" appeared over its opening notes. Since we continually returned to the same spot I found it simpler to play by memory than turn the pages. But in his ignorance he repeatedly said, "Go back to ten." This made an unforgettable impression upon me for I found the word *ten* odd and funny in a musical context. Only later with my second teacher did I learn that *ten* meant "ten.," the abbreviation for tenuto.

My second teacher was Sophia Brilliant-Liven, who had been an assistant teacher to Anton Rubinstein at his great music conservatory in Petrograd (now Leningrad). I consider this association, which began just before my tenth year, the beginning of my studies. I worked with her and her husband, who taught me theory, for four years. I studied Scarlatti, Mozart, Bach, Weber, and Beethoven, but very little of the romantic school; I did some Chopin and Mendelssohn, but no Liszt. I also studied later Russian composers such as Arensky and Liapunow. At thirteen, I was entered in the Greater Chicago Piano Playing Tournament, along with eighty thousand other children. There were three age divisions, and my teacher tried to enter me in the oldest group because she knew I could easily play the required works of the most advanced division. However, her request was turned down, so I had to play in the middle division, which was my age group. Each contestant in this class was required to play the two-part D Major Invention by Bach and a work of one's own choice, mine being Weber's *Perpetual Motion* (it was not really mine but, rather, that of my teacher). As you can imagine there were many play-offs because of the large number of entries, but I kept winning and joined the group of some forty semifinalists who would play at Kimball Hall in Chicago in the first auditions to be opened to the public.

On the evening of the semifinals, the packed house was instructed not to applaud after each contestant's performance because the applause would slow down the program too much and because the difference in the amount of applause might be prejudicial. We drew numbers and performed in the order that our number called for. I drew a very high number so, although the performances began at seven in the evening, it was after eleven when my turn came. The first thing I did was change chairs. The one at the piano was too low for me and, since there were other chairs on the stage, I simply picked one more to my liking. I was the only one who had done this and, while at the time it was the most natural action and didn't seem significant, as I looked back at it later, I realized that it was my first public act as an individual. A professional artist, to be successful, must have individuality of style, individuality of focus. Only through individuality will the artist have something to say that has meaning. Further, I believe such individuality is inborn; the real artist must be as unconscious of his or her individuality as I was on that night when I changed chairs. This is true individuality. It is not gimmicky or consciously planned idiosyncrasy; it emerges from a valid subconscious source.

Having selected a chair that suited me, I sat down and began to play; but I don't remember anything else. I know I must have played through the Bach and gone on to Weber's *Perpetual Motion*. Each one of us was allotted the same amount of time to play and, at the end of that time, the judges rang a bell and we had to stop, no matter where we were in the music. I suddenly heard the bell and came to, realizing that I was nearing the end of the *Perpetual Motion*. I had not been aware of anything from the moment I sat down until the sound of that bell. And in spite of the producer's admonition, the audience burst into such applause that it seemed the walls would crack from the power of the vibration. I still get a chill when I talk about it or recall it because I can even now feel the impact of that applause. It was just tremendous. I won the semifinals and I got my diamond medal, which meant more to me than anything else in the world. I had received a gold medal and other awards in the previous playoffs, but the idea of a diamond medal was just like reaching planet Jupiter.

Yet that evening signified more than the medal; something else even more memorable happened. Mrs. Brilliant-Liven often referred to Anton Rubinstein during her teaching, but never in the same breath with us students. She was very severe in her pedagogy, never complimenting me or showing any approval of what I did. But, the night after the semifinals, she told me that had she been outside the doors of the hall listening to me play she would have thought it was Anton Rubinstein. Such high praise coming from a teacher who never gave it enhanced the value of the diamond medal more than the award of the medal itself could ever be worth. Up until now I had never received any praise from her and, in all truth, I never expected any. She was the teacher, I was the pupil, and it just never occurred to me that I should be praised for doing what was expected. This was the first and only compliment I ever received from her in my four years of study.

Consequently, the winning of the finals was a sort of anticlimax. In my age group the first prize was five hundred dollars and a three-week contract to play in various theaters in Chicago at a salary of between seventy-five and one hundred dollars a week. My family was pleased with my success and with the paid engagements, but they didn't push me; in fact, they never had. Although there never had been any question about my pursuing music as a career, my parents were not aggressive, career-minded, ambitious people at all. They knew, as well as I, that at age nine I was considered a *wunderkind* and had some amount of notoriety, but in no way did they spoil me or make a big fuss over me. They knew I was serious about my music. Succeeding at it was a normal, natural event. I felt no pressure because I knew my direction and the family simply let it lead me. Glamor, exploitation, special attention were out; work was in. Brilliant-Liven and her husband were extremely disciplinary and extremely serious-minded musicians; they never let me forget my purpose. The whole idea was that, as a musician, you just devote all your energies to your work. I had to be a serious student of music, or none at all.

Yet I didn't practice all that much, either; from seventh grade on through high school I spent two to three hours a day at the piano. Otherwise my days were pretty much like any other youngster's. I went to ordinary American public schools, did my studies, and ended up in the upper levels of my classes; now and then I got the very top grades. Then once or twice a week I was excused from the last forty-five minute session of the day so that I could have my music lessons.

I remember one day coming home from a lesson with Brilliant-Liven and telling my mother that I had learned everything I could from that teacher and wanted to go to another one. There was no uproar or outcry about it; we simply went to another teacher, Jan Chiapusso, himself a concert pianist. He had had Western European training, while Brilliant-Liven had studied in the strong Russian tradition. So, while I received my solid Russian foundation stressing technical perfection, singing tone and meticulous musicianship from Brilliant-Liven, I learned from Chiapusso the Western European schools—the Dutch, the German, the French. As well as having studied with various famous Western European performers and teachers, Chiapusso was a Bach scholar and was also well versed in European philosophy, Greek sculpture and art. I discovered that he was a very widely-read and profoundly educated human being, which you do not find too often, with all due respect, in piano teachers, even the very good ones. He was also an experienced concert pianist, having played throughout Europe for many years. I worked with him under full scholarship, as with Brilliant-Liven. With her I'd had one lesson weekly. He offered me two and I moved naturally into the biweekly demands.

At my first lesson, he assigned a Bach prelude and fugue, a work of Beethoven, some Chopin, and several other composers. I returned three days later. Starting the lesson chronologically, I handed him the Bach score. "Do you have it memorized?" he asked. And I replied, "Yes." So he said, "All right, play it." So I played it through and he didn't say a word. Then he asked to hear the other works, and I went on with them. Again he said nothing but assigned another prelude and fugue to me. I left and came back three or four days later for the second lesson of the week. I started the lesson the same way, handing him the new Bach score. Again he asked whether I had this memorized too? I told him that I had; he told me to play it. I played it through, and when I finished he said, "My God, girl! If you can do this, you should specialize in Bach." And that was the beginning of that individuality, that focus I spoke of. It was the first time I heard that I was doing anything unusual. I had been learning Bach works with my former teacher for four years with the same speed and she had never once mentioned that it was unique. I didn't know—I didn't realize that Bach was more difficult than Mendelssohn to absorb, memorize, play. I just absorbed it all so quickly, so naturally. From that moment on, I worked continuously with a great deal of Bach repertoire and also began musicological studies. I studied the harpsichord, the clavichord, and the organ. But I didn't do all the work at every lesson. We used to have sessions where for four hours I would listen, and Chiapusso would play through all the late Beethoven sonatas for me. He'd take me through all the Beethoven quartets and, in the course of the lesson, he'd make casual references to Hegel and other philosophers. I was deeply impressed by the copies of great Greek sculpture that decorated the room. I learned that he had been born in Java, of Dutch parents, and although he was taken to Holland at the age of six months, having the kind of inquiring mind he had, he knew all about the gamelan orchestra, the historic traditional orchestra of Java. I learned, at the age of fourteen, a great deal about the gamelan orchestra. That meant I knew all these wonderful sounds of which the gamelan orchestra was capable and the type of music that was written for it. Also, I knew harpsichord sound, I knew clavichord sound, and I knew the touch and technique of these instruments. I knew the organ. Chiapusso used to take me regularly to organ recitals. I studied with him only two years, but this period was the great rich fertile source of my future life.

There is no question about his being the greatest musical influence on my life. True, he had some pretty good blotting paper to work with because I absorbed everything he poured out. I'd come to him with a solid foundation, one that could be built upon without tedious reparations. I studied all styles of piano music with him, adding the romantic-virtuoso compositions of Liszt and Chopin, and continued with the whole gamut of standard solo and concerto repertoire for pianists.

At the same time, I was doing specialized studies in Bach, not only the music of Bach, but the style, the instruments, the history, the sonorities, and pre-Bach music. This all-embracing study also included the styles of the transcribers of Bach, such as Busoni, D'Albert, and Liszt. Furthermore, because the piano as an instrument has changed over the years, I had to learn how to relate Bach to the instruments of his time as well as to the contemporary instrument. The concept of sound was becoming a vital element in my musical education. I have not forgotten what I learned about the gamelan orchestra either. Additionally I recall that Brilliant-Liven had taken me to a concert at Orchestra Hall in Chicago when I was ten years old in which Leon Theremin, the great inventor of electronic instruments, gave a concert of all electronic instruments. The sounds were quite thrilling and unforgettable to me. All this was woven into the very fabric of my studies of music, performance styles and techniques.

The decision to try out for the Juilliard School was rather sudden. Only one prelude and fugue by Bach was required for the audition; I had so many prepared that I listed them on paper rather than giving a long verbal recitation of my prepared repertoire. In addition to these, I fulfilled the other requirements with Beethoven's Sonata, Opus 2, No. 2, Chopin's G Minor Ballade, Liszt's *La Campanella,* and an additional extra work, the Bach-Busoni *Chaconne.* At the time I appeared at the New York audition, the faculty of Juilliard was composed of Alexander Siloti, Joseph and Rosina Lhevinne, Olga Samaroff, Carl Friedberg, Ernest Hutcheson, and James Friskin—all great and world-famous pianists. Mr. Hutcheson read off my written list to the judges saying, "Which prelude and fugue would you like to hear?" To my surprise I find in recent years that this query has become legendary and I meet people everywhere in the queue backstage following my concerts asking if this is true. It is true.

I also performed, at the judges' request, some of the Beethoven sonata, the Chopin, and the Liszt. I won the fellowship and Olga Samaroff became my new teacher. Due to my own interest in continuing work on Bach, I learned three preludes and fugues a week in order to complete the entire forty-eight. Every Monday I'd start a new set; on Friday I'd bring in the three preludes and fugues memorized and worked out in interpretation. To these were added other music such as a Beethoven sonata, some Ravel, Chopin, part of a concerto, etc. Samaroff did little about technical development for me, but her great sense of projecting music out to the listener and her fine sense of harmony were her chief contributions to my studies.

Within two months, just before my seventeenth birthday, I had a very great experience. On a Wednesday afternoon in early December, I began a new prelude and fugue, the A Minor from Book One, which was among those I planned to play at the Friday lesson. It's a very difficult work and I realized its complexity immediately. I started work and suddenly lost consciousness. I don't know for how long, whether it was a split second or half an hour, but I do know that, when I came to, I had an insight into Bach's structure, his musical psychology, his sense of form, with an entirely new concept which emerged from the necessities of the musical sources and original structures as Bach composed them. At the same time, I knew that I had to create an entirely new technique for playing the piano to parallel this whole new concept of Bach's music. I knew what I had to do and why I had to do it, for the power of my perception arose from the very music itself. It had no association with any fashion of Bach performance, approved or otherwise; I was well enough educated in the field to know these. My experience emerged from perhaps the most pure objective kind of insight that I can imagine.

About the *causes* of moving from consciousness into the unconscious state of experience and the attendant new insights I can

Rosalyn Tureck as conductor and performer

tell you very little, simply because I don't know what the causes are. And who does, really, beyond the privilege of the experience itself? I personally know other people, particularly great creative scientists, who have experienced this phenomenon also, and I've heard them talk about it and have discussed our common experiences with them. My scientist friends have also experienced similar loss of consciousness and perceived a new hypothesis or formulation clearly; then they spent years developing it and refining the techniques which prove it. Several of my friends were Nobel Prize winners as a result of the insights produced by this kind of experience. It seems that such revelations came after very hard work and deep concentration about a particular problem that defied solution. Just why and how, no one seems to know. But I did know this: I could not go back to my old way of playing Bach, even though it was a very much approved and accepted way of playing.

I had gone through a door into a new world and, strangely enough, I had no doubt about the importance and significance of what I had found or what I would do. Yet, although Samaroff approved vigorously of what I had found and done, she doubted that it was possible that it could be done at all outside of occasional applications. I knew my foundation had been solid. Brilliant-Liven and Jan Chiapusso had given me a deep, broad, and rich background in all phases of keyboard techniques and music. Chiapusso's influence was especially valuable because of the musicological and instrumental concentration on Bach. For two years, at ages fifteen and sixteen, I had played all-Bach recitals in Chicago. In some way, all this training was a foundation for subconscious efforts which caused my new insight. So I began work, as a result of my new insights, in a totally new way. I'd never heard anyone play Bach as I now attempted to, and it was so difficult physically and mentally that, in the case of the particular fugue which catapulted me into a new world of thought and discovery, it took me two whole days to learn four lines.

This doesn't mean, however, that I abandoned my studies with Samaroff. I continually enlarged my repertoire in all the standard literature. It was my approach to Bach that changed. I kept working at a wholly new technique in playing Bach on the piano and a wholly different intellectual process. It is a process of thought that pianists ordinarily do not experience because their intellectual processes, often unconscious ones, are concerned with music that is composed as a result of an entirely different fundamental musical and structural concept. They are more often involved with the forms which grew from emphasis on the harmonic system, for instance, sonata form, so prominent in the late eighteenth and the nineteenth centuries.

My fingering apparatus underwent changes, too. Each of my ten fingers is totally independent and capable of doing something different from the other every split second I'm playing. This constitutes one important aspect of the multileveled insights which I experienced. It meant developing a totally different technical approach which demanded uncompromising control of every single finger. Each finger must be capable of every type of touch while every other finger is doing another type of touch simultaneously. The dynamics must be such that a different quantity of tone can be produced at different levels of playing so that the texture and quality of tone, although different for each finger, can be interrelated and can blend in the different motifs that are going on simultaneously. The fingers' touch, tonal quantity and quality must relate as the lines move horizontally and contrapuntally to each other as, for example, in a four-voiced fugue; they must relate harmonically as they move in a harmonic progression from one section to another; even within short phrases they must relate contrapuntally and harmonically so that, although each phrase, long or short, is an entity in itself, the differences in touch create a complete unified structure. This is a microscopic view of my technical style for a Bach performance on the piano.

Now this is not what's known as nineteenth- or twentieth-century piano technique. I am against using modern piano technique in playing Bach, because modern piano technique is based on the use of the piano according to our inheritance from the late nineteenth century and as we know it today. That piano is only about a hundred years old; it was the piano of Chopin, of Liszt, Brahms, Scriabin, Tchaikovsky, and Rachmaninoff. It is the piano of the lush, romantic sound of the big virtuoso technique; but in actual fact and historical time it is a limited instrument and occupies a small period of time in musical history. The piano has changed greatly from the time that it was born, and it is changing continually. It has changed in my own lifetime; the piano that I and all of us play today is already different from the pianos of my childhood. Composers are writing for today's piano in a different way from those of seventy-five years ago.

Composers' concepts have in turn influenced piano techniques and sonorities. Artists and critics who are against the piano for Bach are in error when they adversely criticize the piano for Bach performance for they are talking about today's piano and today's piano techniques and sound. Bach knew the piano; in fact, about ten years ago, a

scholar produced evidence that Bach was a salesman for the Silber-
mann piano. It was sold to a Polish count and a copy of the receipt is
in existence. Bach's famous composition, *The Musical Offering,* was
composed after his visit to Frederick the Great, who possessed a
number of pianos. It has been shown that Bach conceived the keyboard part of the Trio Sonata for piano, not for a harpsichord. So
scholarship has changed the picture in this respect. Therefore, those
who had insisted that Bach be played only on the harpsichord and
those who play *The Musical Offering* keyboard part on the harpsichord have been playing it on the "wrong" instrument; they should
have been playing it on the piano.

Of course, the piano of Bach's time, the piano that Bach knew, was
different from the piano of today, just as it is different from the piano
of Beethoven, Chopin, Prokofieff, Stravinsky, Boulez. These instruments require fundamentally different techniques from each other,
different mental conceptions, different structural conceptions, different sonority conceptions. So the use of the term *piano* may be con-
fined in a limited way to only one of these periods. But the piano
deserves better than to be thought of in limited terms. Realizing this,
I had to create a new technique of playing the piano in order to bring
forth the structures of Bach. I also recognized that these structures
couldn't just pop out of a personal whim or solely subjective ideas.
So I worked from the very structure of the music itself.

The result is I do what Bach tells me to do. I never tell the music
what to do, I never make the decision; it—the music—makes the
decision. But you have to go very deep into the score. You can't just
use your eyes; you have to use many more faculties. And you must
be a total scholar, as comprehensive as possible. With me, it started
at the age of fourteen when I began studies in musicology. My research has continued throughout my entire life. I have worked in the
field of embellishment, which is one of the major areas in which you
have to be thoroughly, deeply, widely versed before you should dare
to play any major work of Bach either on the harpsichord or on any
other instrument. One must thoroughly know and understand embellishment performance practices. It's a life study in itself.

Besides embellishment, the study of antique instruments and historical performance practices have gradually come to the fore in musicological studies. Until fairly recently, the study of manuscripts, instruments, and instrument making received greatest emphasis. Now historical performance practice is a very important area of musicological study, namely, studying the notations and treatises of composers and scholars of the period and their performance approaches to the different instruments of the time. This is an area in which I have spent my life. I have been steeped in it and have never ceased my historical studies in spite of all the busy demands of my career, the glamor of success and international tours. And I am immersed in my scholarly work as deeply now as I have always been and always will be. I recently gave two lectures at Columbia University where I was introduced by the chairman of the music department as "a scholar and an artist, and the unique liaison of the two." I am grateful for this compliment; the amalgamation has indeed been the working style of my life.

Naturally, I haven't neglected the performance aspect of my career. But I'll have to retrace my steps a bit. In my fourth year at Juilliard, I never intended to make my mature career debut until I was thirty. I didn't think an artist was really fully matured short of the kind of background and general experience that more years contribute. I wasn't interested in splashing out in a flashy career. I was a musician and a scholar and a serious performer and I didn't want to rush into the limelight, and I didn't feel the need to do so. But my teacher placed me in two contests: one was the Naumburg Contest, which gave a Town Hall performance debut for its prize. Of course, in those days, Town Hall was the great recital hall for the soloist. The other was the combined Schubert Memorial and National Federation of Music Clubs Contest. For the Naumberg Contest, I presented an all-Bach program and I came up to the finals and I lost. The first and only contest I'd ever lost! The judges said they couldn't possibly give me the prize because nobody could make a career in Bach. Very shortly after, I was entered into the other contest, but it was against my will. I did not wish to enter the contest; I had no expectation nor wish for an early public career, so it never even occurred to me to enter the contest. However, among other things, my reluctant entry gave rise to a very moving human experience.

We always had our Juilliard examinations in the spring because the fellowship recommenced the next autumn. There were people who, rejected after the first year, never returned. If you survived three years, you were given a letter saying you may now be considered a graduate of the Juilliard Graduate School and that letter was more important, in those days, than any university degree. So you had to survive at least three years. But some outstanding people were allowed to stay on longer and were granted a fellowship for additional years. When I was at the end of my third year, there was no problem about that; I got the fellowship for the next year. But just at the time of my third year examination, I remember meeting one afternoon with one of the most remarkable pianists of the school. He was one of the older students and very experienced. He'd already played many concerts professionally and was preparing to make his formal debut in New York. His program was fully planned and he'd worked on it the whole previous year. He played this program at his spring examinations for the faculty and informed them that he was hoping to make his debut with that program. We ran into each other in the corridor shortly after his examination and he offered to buy me an ice cream soda because he had something very exciting to tell me.

While we were having our ice cream, he told me of his experience at his exam. He said that, after playing his program, the faculty told him that it was silly to spend his own money on a Town Hall debut. They thought he was so remarkable that he should enter this huge contest. It was held only once every two years because the prizes were so great that both sponsoring groups felt that a high enough level of talent was not easily available every year. The contest was sponsored in order to give major recognition to a really remarkable young pianist and to provide a debut on the highest level. The faculty advised him to enter this contest because they thought he had a tremendous chance of winning. It wouldn't take place until the next spring, so he'd have to wait a year, but they thought the delay would be worth it since he was so eligible for the award. He was very thrilled, of course, to hear this kind of opinion of his work. Over the soda, I told him how thrilled I was for him and that nothing could be better. And when I finished he said, "Now Rosalyn, don't *you* enter that contest!" Well, I looked at him and I just laughed; I was nineteen years old, and he was in his late twenties. To me, at the age of nineteen, the late twenties seemed generations away, very old. So I laughed and told him that I wouldn't dream of entering the contest. "I am not ready; I don't want to make my debut for a least another ten or twelve years," I told him. And I just forgot about the whole thing. The next winter, late in the winter, my teacher suddenly told me that I was to enter this contest. I replied that the proposal was ridiculous. I wasn't even prepared. I was to have three concertos and two recital programs plus certain specific required works. Six weeks before the first play-off I still hadn't signed the entry forms. I had continually neglected to bring in the application which my teacher had to sign. Then one afternoon I came in for my lesson, and she had the application which she had signed and she said, "Now you sign!" So I signed with resignation and then I hurriedly started work at the required compositions and concertos so as to be prepared for the first play-off which was only six weeks away.

I'd certainly forgotten all about the conversation I'd had over the soda the previous spring. I arrived for the New York State auditions, which were being held at Steinway Hall; a studio for each entrant was assigned for warming up. I was still memorizing one of the Beethoven sonatas, in fact, so I went up to my studio and practiced like a slave until it was my turn to come down and play. We had two play-offs, one with a screen in front of us and one without. Since that play-off was for New York State, many Juilliard students were entered; in fact, I believe *all* the entrants were from Juilliard. I remember that, on coming into Steinway Hall, I saw the young man I spoke of earlier; suddenly the whole conversation of a year ago came back to me. I felt shaky at the sight of him, but I didn't have the slightest expectation of winning anyway so I wasn't too concerned. Well, I won; I won the New York State context, and that meant this fellow was out immediately.

He disappeared for two days and two nights. Nobody knew where he was, and many thought he'd committed suicide. But he fortunately hadn't. For some years he did go on; he played at Town Hall and he gave concerts. Eventually he turned to teaching. I remember telling him after I won that I was sorry. I hadn't expected to enter at all, but

I had been placed over my own protestations in this contest. I also asked him to forgive me. He was gentle. There was no dramatic, terrible scene at all; but we never saw each other again. I don't know whether he ever forgave me or not. It would have helped had there been a second prize, but there wasn't because this was the first play-off, the state auditions.

The next was the district auditions including several states. As it happened I played against only one person. He was a student from Curtis Institute, a very experienced pianist in his late twenties. Everybody at Juilliard said that he was a "professional." I still regarded myself as a student. I won that play-off, too, and I'll never forget the next day when I came into the Juilliard cafeteria for lunch. The whole cafeteria got up and applauded me because, as they saw it, I'd won for the Juilliard School. I went on to the semifinals which included all national district winners, and then the finals, and I won the double prize of the Schubert Memorial and National Federation of Music Clubs. I was twenty years old. This had nothing to do with Bach; I won it on a varied pianistic repertoire. A major manager took me on immediately, I played at Carnegie Hall, and had a career on my hands at the age of twenty. That's how my entry into the public music came about—totally unexpectedly and unplanned. In retrospect I must say that, once I began winning, it got rather exciting and it was all very thrilling. After a while though, I had no control over this at all. I had concerts, I had a manager, I started to play everywhere. It was difficult because I had to absorb a large amount of repertoire in order to fulfill continual concert demands and at the same time travel constantly. I found I was learning my concertos on the way to the concert.

Sometimes all the rushing and pressure lead to nervousness, but this is part of the public performer's life. At other times, things went very calmly. In my debut, I played first at Carnegie Hall with Ormandy and the Philadelphia Orchestra, and then a few days later in Philadelphia. By the way, it was with the Brahms B-flat Concerto that I made my debut. New York was followed by two performances in Philadelphia and, by the time I played the second, I found myself yawning in the car on the way to the hall because I was so relaxed. I played the performance and apparently it went very well; but I was not satisfied because I felt that I had gone at it almost too easily before this great audience at the academy. Right then I realized that one must warm one's self psychologically to a certain peak. I would have to become charged up, like a new battery in order to give my fullest. I gave, I played well, but I said, "No, you have to be on a very high level of feeling; you cannot be in a normal, daily state of mind."

I am very aware of the audience. My goal as a performer is not simply to perform or play beautifully and have success. I hope that the experience within myself may give others who are listening some new sense of life. Even if one person in the whole audience has had a new glimmering of an inner vision, an opening of horizons in some way, then it will all be worthwhile. This is my goal for every performance, my chief goal. All the others, to play beautifully and with the greatest sincerity, are means to contribute to my focus on the inner experience—which art is.

Of course I feel gratification when there are those who see deeper into my techniques, into my concepts of the music. These are all based on pure concept—pure concept which I express in music, but which is of itself so abstract that it can be expressed in many other areas of work. To this extent I find myself in sympathetic understanding with biologists, mathematicians, chemists, and physicists. If I leave a legacy, it will be one which rests on a good number of different levels. It will be performance; it will be my style of playing Bach on the piano, my performance on the harpsichord and the clavichord also, perhaps even on electronic instruments; and it will be in the field of scholarship and teaching, as well. But the legacy will I hope be wider on the conceptual level as it pursues the meaning of the amalgamation and the integration of all these different disciplines. It may go still deeper reaching the level of the various conceptualizations that man has realized through history. These manifest themselves in different media and different disciplines. The important thing is the concept out of which emerges a particular art and culture. I'm interested in the fundamental concepts out of which each culture emerges. It's there that my fire burns and heats the lava that wells up and up and over the top of the volcano spilling over the very edges of the crater into external expression.

My work is very diversified. Sometimes I'm at my desk working on a book or on an article; at other times I'm going through the daily business of correspondence, telephone calls, and plans for the next two or three years. Then there's reading, but this is always done at odd moments before sleep or on planes. As you can see from the collection of books I've amassed over the years, the subject matter covers philosophy, literature, art, science, etc. The collection includes almost any subject you can think of. They all deepen my perspective of life in some way. Next, my great love is nature, especially the sky. I walk in the countryside whenever I can because I can see the sky so much more clearly there. Much as I would like to have enjoyed sports, I never indulged in any except on occasional moments because of possible injury to the hands. The only exception to this is swimming, although I'm certainly not the world's greatest. Snorkeling, for me, is a fantastic activity because I see such variety of life under the sea. I have done snorkeling in the Mediterranean, in the south of France. It's another world, and it gives me a great sense of the immensity and the individuality of nature. When I first saw underwater life, I thought, "My God, what music a composer could have written had he seen this!"

I'm also associated with Oxford University now; I'm an Honorary Life Fellow at St. Hilda's College there, and a Visiting Fellow at the new Wolfson College. I've already spent a nine-month term at Wolfson, but since the fellowship is for three years I still have time ahead of me to work there. These periods are devoted solely to writing—no concerts and very little teaching.

As a musician who believes in the totality of life, I cannot discount the place of marriage in life. I am a widow now. But, in terms of marriage, human relationships, and career, I have not missed out on a personal life. I am sad at having lost my husband. We got on well together and there were no problems as far as careers were concerned. He was a scientist, very sensitive to my work, because he understood the nature of my dedication. As a woman, I feel that it is too bad I had no children of my own. My first husband had two very young children when I married him, so I had the experience of being a mother to them for quite a number of years; we had a beautiful relationship, those children and myself. They grew up with me; I helped develop them; they became my children. That relationship turned full circle later, many years after their father and I were divorced. One of the children's children, in a sense my grandchild, appeared in the queue recently in London at Festival Hall, introduced herself, and told me who she was. I was quite surprised, but as things turned out she, her mother, and I began seeing each other again and we have become good friends. I am proud of them because they are fine and beautiful people; they love music, especially Beethoven and Bach, and they say it's the result of my influence. So I have experienced a mother-child relationship without actually having had my own children. It's been both rewarding and fulfilling.

Women have a physiological as well as psychological desire for nurturing human creatures, whether they be children, a husband, or both. Most women need that experience to fulfill themselves. There have been many girl prodigies, tremendously gifted, but so many of them never fully developed as concert artists. They won contests, made their debuts, and started careers; then they decided to marry, have children, and give up the performing career. Others get discouraged, perhaps sooner than men do, simply because it's very hard going. There's still some male prejudice, or at least a background of prejudice, but it's not as prevalent as it was when I began. When I started my career and throughout my entire childhood and young adulthood as a performer, the greatest compliment that many of the press and musicians as well would pay me was that I played like a man. I could not agree that great qualities belonged only to men, but this attitude was universal and I had to live with it. Today no good critic or journalist would write in this manner.

The changes in attitudes are, of course, directly attributable to the changes in the times. The present period is probably the freest period in all of history, at least for those who are lucky enough to live in open, liberty-oriented societies. Not only is this true for the population generally, but especially for us women. We women are freer today in the United States than at any period in history.

Yet I wouldn't mind going back to a previous era just for a visit with Johann Sebastian Bach. I would be interested greatly in his sense of instruments and sonorities. He set so many of the same compositions for different instruments. His keyboard music is not specified solely for the harpsichord, for Bach was not single-instrument minded. If we met, no doubt we'd talk shop about structure, form, and interpretation. I'd like also to hear his thoughts on the spiritual life and human relationships.

I think it's very clear to most people that we're at the end of the Judeo-Christian civilization, which indeed was a very great civilization and reached a great many peaks in art, in thought, and in science. The twentieth century itself has been a fabulous century, filled with what might be called "miracles"; what man has achieved in this century is almost beyond belief. In that sense, I'm very excited about living in our time. But there are many aspects of this century also which are heartbreaking and full of agony, and this I cannot bear. There has been ugliness, physical, visual, aural—all kinds of ugliness. The decadence is on the increase, which forebodes a very dark, black period lasting a long time, perhaps many centuries. Then, I believe, will come a rebirth as always happens on earth. The achievements that have occurred throughout the last two thousand years will reemerge, but developed with new thoughts, new concepts, new extensions, so that the world will come into an era of civilization that will make our advances seem quite miniscule.

Yes, I'd like to visit Bach; and I enjoy tremendously living right now. I should be most interested to live, if I had my choice for another life in the future, about 850 years from now. I think the human society by that time will have fully recovered and created a new and more advanced way of life, thought, and art.

Fortunately for the lovers of the performing art, especially devotees of Bach, Rosalyn Tureck did not wait eight hundred years to be born and postpone her talent. And if the "dark ages" that she predicts actually do occur, her contributions to the study and the performance of Bach's music should be that one candle that is better to light.

André Watts

ANDRÉ WATTS

Dressed for work in casual, loose-fitting slacks and an open-collared sport shirt, André Watts stood in the hall outside his suite at the Sheraton Northbrook on a hot afternoon in July, just one day before he was scheduled to play the Liszt Totentanz *and the Franck* Symphonic Variations *at Ravinia. He usually releases his tensions by doing yoga exercises, but today he took his break by puffing on a giant Havana cigar in the corridor.*

The light inside the suite revealed a slender, handsome man in his thirties. He was cordial, offering tea from the large pot that stood on a table in the living room. A fervent tea drinker himself, he poured the first of many cups that would accompany our conversation.

He speaks in a resonant baritone voice that reveals a faint accent. An articulate man, his excellent English is generously laced with slang and the sometimes colorful language of a man as well acquainted with the rougher side of life as with the amenities of the drawing room. When he ponders a question, his high forehead turns into a grill of furrows that seems to deepen with the depth of his thought. Everything about him, his serious expression, his considerate manners, and general bearing make him seem older than he is.

Because he had burst with such wild acclaim on the concert scene, Watts wasn't quite sure how one pinpointed the causes of success— whether it was his own or someone else's. Although he frequently mentions luck as a factor in the achievements of a successful artist, the fact of his extraordinary talent gives cause to the notion that, like Liszt, he must have been born with the physical ability to manage the instrument, the mental equipment to master it and the emotional drive to express himself through it. His presence bears this out, for Watts is to a concert stage as lightning is to tinder. Explosive. More than any other pianist, his performances are reminiscent of what a Liszt concert must have been like: mesmerizing, theatrical, charged with energy. The effect of his interpretations on audiences has become legend and bears the characteristic of a front-rank virtuoso.

He is eager to participate in the give and take of ordinary conversation and shows interest in a surprisingly wide variety of subjects outside of music. There is little doubt that his level of energy and capacity to keep expanding it are contributing factors in his success as an artist. As our conversation began, he tugged at his shirt collar and explained that success is the result of talent, desire, push, luck, and chance.

MAYBE it's just a state of affairs. It just *is*. It's dangerous to think that you're doing something better or worse because, if you would go back some years and put on an all-Schubert recital advertised with Rubinstein and Schnabel as soloists, Rubinstein would probably have the bigger public appeal because I'm not sure that in his younger years he would have paid as much attention to what was in the music. He played for his public because he was such an expansive human being. Schnabel would say that he's playing for Schubert and for himself. But I don't think there's any discrepancy between the two attitudes, because it's a mistake to begin to put a barrier between your giving your all to the public and giving your all to yourself and to the music. It should be no barrier to your playing. Take the situation in which you sit at home and play the G Major Sonata by Schubert. You know that that's a difficult piece for the public to listen to, but if you believe in it you just go under the assumption that they will believe in it. You sit at home and you practice and try in the most pedantic way to understand the music. Once you're past that, for the moment anyway and for this season, you've gotten as much understanding as you're going to get until the next time you relearn the piece, and go on the stage and give.

I'm a big Schnabel fan myself, but I have the impression that in a charming way he got off on the business of playing against the public. He used to write with great amusement about how he went to a town like Phoenix and played Chopin's Twenty-Four Preludes. He said that by the time he had finished, the hall had slowly emptied; he seemed to get a kick out of that. However, I don't think that emptying a hall is a virtue. The challenge there for Schnabel was to play the Twenty-Four Preludes in a small town in that day and age with absolute integrity and fidelity to Chopin, to himself, and also to the audience so that they would understand the performance. Look at all the music they missed because of his attitude. They left because they were bored. I'm sure Chopin never intended his preludes to be boring. I think that sometimes people assume that, if the music is boring, it must be great music. What kind of an attitude is that? Those guys weren't boring. When you play for the public, you have to play the music and interpret it. You won't be boring, and the public will be with you, not against you.

Sure, people have said to me, "Good God, you're only in your thirties and you have it all. How did you do it? Was it drive? Or did it just come your way? Did you look for it, or what?" Well, I guess the answer to all three questions is yes. Yes, I worked and I was pushed too; but there's a funny kind of danger about pushing. The person who best illustrates the paradox is a marvelous violinist whom I've listened to often because, great man that he is, he is so frequently interviewed. I had read an interview in which he stated that he would never push his children. Unfortunately no interviewer I've heard or read has ever followed up on that response by asking this artist whether or not he'd be such a great figure had he not been pushed. I think he was pushed, and that's why you and I can sit here and talk about him. So I'll give a qualified "yes" to the question of pushing youngsters along. I don't want to use an outright "no" because people might take what I say at face value. They won't question what is said. They'll believe what I said just because I said it. After all, so-and-so made that statement. But let's look at it another way: Why in the hell should a seven-year-old kid want to practice when he can be playing outside with his friends? If he has some inclination, some talent, it's necessary to guide him. A parent should find some way of maintaining a greater time span of interest for his endeavor. The parent must be very watchful to guard a big talent because, if he isn't, years from now the youngster will really hate his parents because he's not going to be able to play at all. He'll complain that, if his mother, father, and teacher had made him practice an hour or so a day when he was eight, he probably would have moved on to great things.

I wouldn't be a pianist today if my mother hadn't made me practice. I sometimes balked at doing it, but I always loved to play the piano. Actually I didn't begin my musical studies at the piano; I started with a small violin when I was four, but then my mother introduced me to the piano when I was about seven. Although she gave me piano lessons for only one year, she was responsible for introducing me to the music of the great classic composers. When my father, a career soldier, was transferred back to Philadelphia, I began attending the Musical Academy there. Of course I also went to regular schools, so it was necessary for me to practice in the afternoons after school hours. On days when I wasn't exactly moved to practice, my mother saw to it that I did. Sometimes she tried coaxing me to the piano by relating the careers of famous musicians, hoping perhaps to inspire me to practice. At thirteen, however, I realized the necessity of practice. I still don't really "like" it all the time, but by now it has become second nature.

But if a child has a wild distaste for the piano, I think parents are limited in what they can do. You can force the child, but I'm not so sure that it works. It just doesn't make any sense. There are rare cases in which coercion has had its effect, such as in the career of one famous artist. It's been said that he was locked in an empty room with little food and had to practice a certain number of hours each day before he was allowed to come out. If he were asked his reaction, he'd probably say that he didn't want to do it and it shouldn't be done, but I don't think he'd say that he'd be better off if it hadn't been done, especially now that he's made it as such a big star. Nevertheless, I still believe it's the wrong way to go about it.

Having a big career, being successful, is very much a matter of chance and a matter of luck; I differentiate between the two. Luck is being in the right place at the right time. Leonard Bernstein was an instrumental force in my career and part of my luck. He introduced me on network television when I was chosen to perform the Liszt E-flat Concerto during the Philharmonic's Youth Concert. Then three weeks later he called and asked me to substitute for Glenn Gould, the scheduled soloist for the Philharmonic's subscription concert, who had become ill. I was very much surprised when I received that call. It all happened so suddenly, it never occurred to me that if I blew it here, I could kiss my career goodbye. This was my big chance; yet, at the time, I simply thought of it all as being fun and exciting. And so I simply played the best I could, and it turned out quite well. Bernstein was definitely responsible for my performing better than I might have ordinarily. The audience went wild and I received something like an eight-minute standing ovation.

Chance is a combination of those funny, indefinable qualities that are in the personality at birth. Your children are like you in many ways, but in some small respects they are different. Their edges are different from your edges. Mine happen to be such that make me well suited to this life. I'm an introspective type without at the same time having a closeted personality. I knew what I wanted. I liked the idea of playing the piano. It was sort of fun. I also liked the idea of a career. My mother often talked to me about traveling around the world as a pianist and all the trappings that went with such a life. And I thought it sounded great. It was work and pleasure at the same time. Yet I had a sort of basic reflex or response to things. I used to be embarrassed by the fact that some events or occurrences got to me. Playing with Bernstein, for instance, I had no thoughts about that performance as the sum total of my life or that, if I failed, I might be kissing my career goodbye.

Then, too, in a career there are many things which I believe people take credit for, but shouldn't. If they do, they're just fooling themselves. Some attributes are inborn; they can be squashed or developed. Sometimes they develop almost without effort on the part of

André Watts practicing

the individual; they just grow with you. I have something like that in me that I'm now happy about but don't dwell on much. I trust myself and my instincts, and it's stood me in very good stead. There are pianists who can be made to sit and practice eight or ten hours a day for years, but nothing's ever going to come of it. The longer you live, the more you realize that environment, temperament, personality, physical and mental constitution are special contributions to the making of a pianist. But of special importance is the ability to analyze situations vis-à-vis oneself, because without it there's no career.

When I received all the acclaim after substituting for Gould, it was a fascinating, bewildering time. It took a while to really figure out what had happened. Success sometimes does funny things to people, and a careful watch must be kept lest you take credit from and place blame on the wrong source. I have to be mostly on my guard about myself and my reaction to success. The main thing is to be honest with one-self. You have to admit all the good and all the bad to yourself so that you know who you are. It's a lot easier to be aware of your iden-tity if you're living on a corn farm in Iowa. The danger in being an idol is thinking you cannot do any wrong. Yet sometimes you do nothing *but* wrong.

Perhaps all this has contributed to my fairly private existence. Al-though I have good friends, I'm not known as an extrovert socializer. My career is a demanding one and so there just isn't enough time for a busy social life. One of my greatest satisfactions is performing; but when I'm not, I like to spend my free moments reading and listening to recordings.

As far as critics are concerned, I've had various attitudes on what's been written about my performances. During the last few years, I have received some of the best and some of the worst reviews; and often, in places where they tore me apart, I really had played well. I think an ideal review should have a constant byline for the reader which would always begin at the top with the words, "Bear in mind that this is but one man's opinion."

Despite his reputation as an independent and a self-styled "loner," Watts doesn't find getting along with conductors very difficult; but problems can arise when he thinks the maestro is unsure of himself.

It's a question of whether or not there's a meeting of minds. At the risk of sounding arrogant, I'm a very good accompanist, and I do a lot of accompanying in my concerts with orchestra, so I'm able to ob-tain what I want most of the time with the conductor even if we don't always quite agree. Problems arise, though, if you work with a con-ductor who gives the impression that he's not one of the really gifted people in the profession; it's far better if he doesn't even try to be helpful because then at least the virtuoso can generate some electricity in the performance. If you have to play with a conductor who is not very gifted but tries to help anyway by telling you to just play and he'll follow you, you as soloist have nowhere to go musically because you simply aren't making any music. All he's trying to do is listen to the beat and bring the orchestra in at the right places; and there are a few conductors who aren't even good at that, so nothing works right and the concert's a disaster.

Ordinarily, I try to learn something from every performance and I'm certainly most willing to be open-minded to things a conductor suggests. For example, I remember when I first started playing the Tchaikovsky B-flat Concerto in concert, the young conductor came up with an idea for dynamics. Although it was written in the score, I'd never done it that way nor had I ever heard of it being done that way. At first I thought, "You really don't want me to do it this way, do you?" But he felt rather insistent about doing it this way; so I thought, "Let's give it a try because it's not going to ruin my idea." We tried it and it actually turned out quite well. At the second performance we bent his idea just a bit and it was very special. That really was a satisfying experience, I must admit.

I don't mean to imply that artists and conductors today don't have their egos; they do, but the behavior resulting from them is different from what it used to be. Hofmann, for instance, had an enormous ego and so did Fritz Reiner; but they got along. Sometimes their remarks sounded like left-handed compliments. Hofmann proclaimed that Reiner was the only conductor he couldn't lose, as if it were Hofmann's intent to confuse conductors. He probably did, but not in a vicious way. There always seemed to be a twinkle in the eye along with the confusion. Rosenthal was another musician who kept the gleam in his eye; there was never a real thrust of the knife, but rather a kind of musical fencing.

Today the egos still manifest themselves, but in strange ways. The virtuoso and the conductor have the phenomenal ego of their predecessors, yet from some mistaken sense of propriety they try to camouflage it. But it shows nevertheless. Let me give you an example. I attended a recital of a pianist who doesn't really have a big American career. He's not a friend of mine, but we know each other well enough to extend a hello. Years ago I went to his debut in New York, and it was a hair-raising experience. First of all I got the giggles, not in hilarity, but because I was so tickled by his performance. He played Schumann's Fantasia, and he played it in the real way; at the end of his performance, he played one of the Liszt rhapsodies, ripping off the glissandi, sitting way back and very straight. He was like a magician and I commented to a friend with me that this was a fantastic performance. After the recital, I went backstage to pay my respects and to tell him what a great performance I thought he gave. Looking around me I saw some of my colleagues with teeth gritted murmuring, "Marvelous concert." It was really killing them that he was so good.

I don't get that at all. These murmurers were pianists who had nothing to fear. They had their careers. Their names were plastered on billboards all over the world. What were they so unhappy about? They should have been content and they should have enjoyed it. They had secure positions but had no security, you know. It's very strange to me, this inability to be convinced that someone else can do well and should be told how delightful the performance was. Each one develops his own style of playing, and no one can take away what you have, nor is anyone threatening you. Sure, you can look around and find someone who seventy percent of the time plays badly and still makes more money than you do. So what? If you're not starving, why should you bother? It's a waste of good energy to be bitter about it.

I suppose the narrowness of some musicians in society today has something to do with it. It wasn't always like that, though. Look at the time of Liszt. Liszt really had *chutzpah*. He was a fantastic musician, well read, innovative, and an individual who could really hold people. And he was very generous, particularly of his time and talent. The way careers are set up now, means that you have to make a career early. It's too true that, if you don't have that concert, someone else will and you may never get it again. That's sort of a pity. I would have enjoyed living in Liszt's time, but I wouldn't say I'd rather have lived then. I'm here, now, and that's fine with me.

I find it exciting to perform for audiences. Although you may not notice the audience, actively that is, you know it's there. And there are two ways of looking at playing concerts. Of course every performer is nervous before a concert, and one way to occupy your mind is to think of failure. If you fail, you think, it's bad for your career and the future of your concerts; so you can be very strained and feel almost hostile toward the people out there because some of them might be waiting for you to mess up.

On the other hand, you can take the attitude I prefer, which is to prepare the programs, go on stage, and proffer your music to the audience. I try to avoid expecting too much from the public and just play in the most open way I can. But a concert always is an incredible exposition of one's daring and insides. If you're not willing to do that, or if you feel uncomfortable about it, then there's a limit to what you can offer the people. Sometimes when I come on stage I find myself saying "Hello" under my breath as I bow. It may seem silly and ridiculous, but that's how I feel.

There is a certain nervousness that is almost always there. It usually won't crop up in the middle of a performance unless things are going badly. Each person then has to work this out for himself. Generally, nervousness for me is a matter of degree. I've played a fair number of years now, and the public will always be the same in that respect. So the nervousness is in me, but it's not constant. I've had whole seasons where I find I'm always nervous; then there are times when everything flows smoothly. About eight or nine years ago, I had a season of almost nothing but memory lapses which sort of became a cycle. I knew I had a memory failure in a previous concert, so I waited for one in the present performance. It went on and on. Eventually it passed and, even though now occasionally I have a memory lapse, nothing ever equaled that particular year. Sometimes the rehearsals are good, sometimes bad, but a bad rehearsal doesn't necessarily forecast a poor performance. It depends on what was bad about the rehearsal. A performer has to learn to live with cases of nerves. It may be the program, the hall, the conductor, or anything else. But the artist must work it out for himself.

A great musician friend of mine once remarked to me that he

thought people never play *differently,* only better or worse. And I wanted to immediately disagree with him. Yet, as I thought about what he had said, I began thinking that it might be true. Although we hope to become more knowledgeable and play with greater maturity, the core, the basic thrust of the attitude toward music, remains the same. It's an interesting thought for the musician to ponder, isn't it?

INDEX